"Historians of culture and of sci figure in the transition from the Many idealize (or even idolize) him, and some demonize him, generally for the same thing—his philosophy of science that has become dominant in the English-speaking world (ostensibly a Christian approach to science). Here Dr. Innes provides us with a study of the man's own writings that shows both appreciation and incisive critique; he especially helps us to see how Bacon's approach—whatever positive things we may say about it—contributed to the secularization of the Western world, and thus to its dehumanization. He also opens the way for a more genuinely Christian and humane philosophy of science. For all this I thank Dr. Innes!"

— **C. John Collins**, Professor of Old Testament, Covenant Theological Seminary; author, *The God of Miracles: An Exegetical Examination of God's Action in the World* and *Science and Faith: Friends or Foes?*

"*Francis Bacon* is an excellent brief introduction to Bacon's revolutionary project. David Innes gets it: Bacon's innovative experimentalism; a new hope for worldly progress dissembled under a pseudo-Christianity; a 'total reconstruction' of knowing and arts extending to morals, politics, and especially religion. Innes chronicles all this in short and lively sentences peppered with original observations and conveying serious scholarship. He addresses the contemporary underestimation of Bacon, entertains alternative views (while overawed by none), acknowledges obvious benefits of modern science, and corrects the prevailing translations. Besides, Innes is seriously moral and devout. He raises difficulties with the value-relativism of scientism and the distractions and temptations of the technological outlook—difficulties that beset us all."

— **Robert K. Faulkner**, Research Professor, Boston College; author, *Francis Bacon and the Project of Progress*

"David C. Innes gives an insightful analysis of the sixteenth-century thinker Francis Bacon, whose vision was foundational to the rise of empirical science and technology. Indeed, Baconianism has become part of the very intellectual air we breathe, which is why it is crucial for Christians to think critically about Bacon's influence—both on Western culture and on our own thinking. Innes skillfully disentangles the elements in Bacon's thought that are compatible with biblical truth (he did, after all, work within a largely Christian intellectual milieu) from the elements that are contrary to biblical truth, and therefore destructive both personally and socially. That is not an easy job because Bacon often obfuscates to hide his more secular ideas from the uninitiated. Innes is a reliable guide, and this book will be especially helpful to readers concerned about how science and technology have shaped the modern worldview."

> —**Nancy R. Pearcey**, Professor of Apologetics and Scholar-in-Residence, Houston Baptist University; author, *Total Truth: Liberating Christianity from Its Cultural Captivity*; coauthor, *The Soul of Science: Christian Faith and Natural Philosophy*

"Francis Bacon is a key figure in introducing a new way of thinking about the world, at the heart of which is optimistic reliance on scientific method. David Innes has given us a nuanced, thoughtful, and critical introduction to Francis Bacon, in his life and thought. His book moves from Bacon's views to assess the larger issues about science and its dominating role in modern aspirations for knowledge, power, and happiness. I heartily recommend the book as a path for rethinking the role of science from a Christian point of view."

> —**Vern S. Poythress**, Professor of New Testament, Westminster Theological Seminary; author, *Redeeming Science: A God-Centered Approach*

"Fascinating study of the controversial role played by Francis Bacon in fashioning the worldview of modern science. While keenly appreciating the many benefits of science and technology, Innes probes the darker side of Bacon's thought that helped give rise to a scientific enterprise largely unbound by moral restraint. Subtle, provocative, and exquisitely relevant to our current culture."

—**John G. West**, Vice President, Discovery Institute; editor, *The Magician's Twin: C. S. Lewis on Science, Scientism, and Society*; author, *Darwin Day in America: How Our Politics and Culture Have Been Dehumanized in the Name of Science*

"More than merely 'the herald of modern philosophy,' as some have dubbed him, Francis Bacon was really the chief architect of modernism, with its scientism and resultant technological society. David Innes reveals how this is so in a clear and compelling way in his new volume on Bacon in P&R's Great Thinkers series. Innes notes in the very first paragraph of his work that 'we live in Bacon's world. He planned it all, and we participate unwittingly in his grand project.' Thus he motivates this insightful exploration and critique of Bacon's great project of reconstructing all learning and society on the foundation of his new empirical scientific methodology. As the exploration unfolds, we discover underneath the veneer of Christianity in Bacon's work the subtle but potent subversion and domestication of Christianity to serve the purposes of Bacon's very this-worldly vision. Innes proves to be an excellent guide, charitably appreciative of the good and true in Bacon's work and at the same time incisive in his criticism of what is in fact inimical to the Christian faith. He connects the dots to our own time, showing how the world in which we live today has been significantly shaped by Bacon's original vision. He drills down to Bacon's presuppositions, exposing the source of Bacon's subversive project. And he gives wise advice for faithful

Christian engagement with Bacon's thought and its influence in our society, including a blueprint for developing a godly science. This book will be a blessing to both the church and the academy in the world of Bacon's grand project. I highly recommend it to all who long for the advancement of the kingdom of God."

    —**John Wingard**, Professor of Philosophy and Dean of Humanities, Covenant College

Francis

BACON

GREAT THINKERS

A Series

Series Editor
Nathan D. Shannon

Francis
BACON

David C. Innes

P&R
PUBLISHING
P.O. BOX 817 • PHILLIPSBURG • NEW JERSEY 08865-0817

"Let us set out to build a truer knowledge of ourselves and our fellowmen, to work for tolerance and understanding among the nations and to use the tremendous forces of science and learning for the betterment of man's lot upon this earth."
—Queen Elizabeth's Christmas Broadcast, 1952

"We will restore science to its rightful place, and wield technology's wonders to raise health care's quality and lower its cost. We will harness the sun and the winds and the soil to fuel our cars and run our factories. And we will transform our schools and colleges and universities to meet the demands of a new age. All this we can do. And all this we will do."
—Barack H. Obama's First Inaugural Address, January 20, 2009

ISBN: 978-1-62995-449-3 (pbk)
ISBN: 978-1-62995-450-9 (Epub)
ISBN: 978-1-62995-451-6 (Mobi)

Printed in the United States of America

Library of Congress Cataloging-in-Publication Data

Names: Innes, David C., 1962- author.
Title: Francis Bacon / David C. Innes.
Description: Phillipsburg [New Jersey] : P&R Publishing, 2019. | Series: Great thinkers | Includes bibliographical references and index.
Identifiers: LCCN 2019012221 | ISBN 9781629954493 (pbk.) | ISBN 9781629954509 (epub) | ISBN 9781629954516 (mobi)
Subjects: LCSH: Bacon, Francis, 1561-1626.
Classification: LCC B1198 .I56 2019 | DDC 192--dc23
LC record available at https://lccn.loc.gov/2019012221

To my father, Leslie G. Innes, the scientist, the master of psychology from King's College, Aberdeen, the model of Scottish enlightenment, whose unconscious example and bejeweled library made serious university study of human things the obvious course for me.

CONTENTS

SERIES INTRODUCTION

Amid the rise and fall of nations and civilizations, the influence of a few great minds has been profound. Some of these remain relatively obscure, even as their thought shapes our world; others have become household names. As we engage our cultural and social contexts as ambassadors and witnesses for Christ, we must identify and test against the Word those thinkers who have so singularly formed the present age.

The Great Thinkers series is designed to meet the need for critically assessing the seminal thoughts of these thinkers. Great Thinkers hosts a colorful roster of authors analyzing primary source material against a background of historical contextual issues, and providing rich theological assessment and response from a Reformed perspective.

Each author was invited to meet a threefold goal, so that each Great Thinkers volume is, first, *academically informed.* The brevity of Great Thinkers volumes sets a premium on each author's command of the subject matter and on the secondary discussions that have shaped each thinker's influence. Our authors identify the most influential features of their thinkers' work and address them with precision and insight. Second, the series maintains a high standard of *biblical and theological faithfulness*. Each volume stands on an epistemic commitment to "the whole counsel of God" (Acts 20:27), and is thereby equipped for fruitful critical engagement. Finally, Great Thinkers texts are *accessible*, not burdened with jargon or unnecessarily difficult vocabulary. The goal is to inform and equip the reader as effectively as possible through clear writing, relevant analysis, and incisive, constructive critique. My hope is that this series will distinguish itself by striking with biblical faithfulness and the riches of the Reformed tradition at the central nerves of culture, cultural history, and intellectual heritage.

Bryce Craig, president of P&R Publishing, deserves hearty thanks for his initiative and encouragement in setting the series in motion and seeing it through. Many thanks as well to P&R's director of academic development, John Hughes, who has assumed, with cool efficiency, nearly every role on the production side of each volume. The Rev. Mark Moser carried much of the burden in the initial design of the series, acquisitions, and editing of the first several volumes. And the expert participation of Amanda Martin, P&R's editorial director, was essential at every turn. I have long admired P&R Publishing's commitment, steadfast now for over eighty-five years, to publishing excellent books promoting biblical understanding and cultural awareness, especially in the area of Christian apologetics. Sincere thanks to P&R, to these fine brothers and sisters, and to several others not mentioned here for the opportunity to serve as editor of the Great Thinkers series.

Nathan D. Shannon
Seoul, Korea

FOREWORD

Practical wisdom, combining learning and common sense, demands an understanding of our own times, so that, like the sons of Issachar, we might know what to do. However, we cannot understand our times by looking on the surface. Current events, trends, data analysis, and innovation cannot help us navigate life in the world today. Learning to make sense of the times into which we have been called requires studying an unfamiliar past while attending to the ends—the purpose, meaning, and state of being of our lives and of life itself.

In this volume, Professor Innes opens the way for us to begin to glimpse Sir Francis Bacon's view of the world, in which he commends the "scientific" method—solving temporal, material problems through applied technology. Bacon's practical aims have reordered our times—by common consent and without objection—effectively to negate serious attention to our past and efficiently to bypass consideration of the established ends of human life, community, and society. In short, Bacon replaced wisdom and virtue with methods and techniques.

Bacon's design has improved real material conditions across

the globe, but it has failed in a profound way. While he succeeded in improving our circumstances, Bacon failed to improve the human condition—and this failure of Bacon's project is just as real and practical as its visible successes. Albert Borgmann calls the empty results of material prosperity fueled by technology "advanced poverty." We feel such poverty in searching anxiety, pressurized depression, and mounting forms of personal emptiness.

In this short book, Innes provides us with an unvarnished look at Bacon's design—a design we see in the methods and techniques that have fashioned our times. Innes presents parameters for deeper understanding of Bacon's work. His work invites us into further study of a sort that delivers keen insight into our own times in ways that are not available through current media sources.

Marshall McLuhan grounded his account of the emergence of electronic media and their effects on the human condition in the words of Psalm 115:

> Their idols are silver and gold,
>> the work of human hands.
> They have mouths, but do not speak;
>> eyes, but do not see.
> They have ears, but do not hear;
>> noses, but do not smell.
> They have hands, but do not feel;
>> feet, but do not walk;
>> and they do not make a sound in their throat.
> Those who make them become like them;
>> so do all who trust in them.

Bacon's design has shifted the attention and energy of the modern world decisively to trust the work of human hands. We can observe and experience the consequences in our times. As Innes traces for us here, studying Francis Bacon exposes the spirit of our own age and bids us to place our trust elsewhere, in the one who "made the heavens and the earth" and who "does all he pleases."

Calvin L. Troup
President and Professor of Communication
Geneva College

PREFACE

The standard collection of Bacon's works is the London edition of *The Works of Francis Bacon*, edited by Spedding, Ellis, and Heath. References to this source will be footnoted as *Works* followed by volume and page number (e.g., *Works* V:421). However, this is inaccessible for most readers, who should have a reasonable hope of looking up references for further investigation. I have, therefore, where possible, cited works that are commonly available.

I refer to *The Great Instauration* by page number in the inexpensive and freely available Hackett collection, *Selected Philosophical Works*, edited by Rose-Mary Sargent (e.g., *GI* 66). I refer to *The New Organon*, also available in the Hackett volume, by Bacon's book and aphorism numbers (e.g., *NO* I.129). Sargent uses the traditional Spedding translation with minor adjustments that she has judged to be helpful for twenty-first-century readers. Where I do not find her changes helpful, I reverse them. I refer to writings in the inexpensive and freely available Oxford World's Classics, *The Major Works*, edited by Brian Vickers (e.g., *MW* 20), but I cite *The Advancement of*

Learning and *New Atlantis* by page numbers in *The Major Works* if the work is named in the body of the text, and by abbreviated name and page number otherwise (e.g., *AL* 147 or *NA* 457). I refer to Bacon's *Essays* simply by essay number (e.g, Essay No. 6). *Thoughts and Conclusions* and *The Masculine Birth of Time* are found only in Benjamin Farrington's book, *The Philosophy of Francis Bacon* (Chicago: University of Chicago Press, 1966) and will be cited as *TC* or *MBT*, respectively, followed by the page number in Farrington (e.g., *TC* 77). For ease of readability, if there are multiple references, they will appear in a footnote.

Sadly, a reliable translation of Bacon's Latin works is not available. For example, Spedding uses "power" to translate *potentiae*, but renders *amplitudinis* as "power" in one place and "greatness" in another, despite the importance of the concept of power in Bacon's thought. This is a frustrating impediment to the serious student of Bacon's thought who relies on a translator. Equally unhelpful is Spedding's rendering of *Instauratio* simply as such in the title and in one other place, but as "reconstruction" in a highly significant passage ("total reconstruction of sciences") without so much as a footnote—which is astonishing, especially since Bacon's *Works* is intended for scholars. Basil Montague's translation has its own problems, and that of Lisa Jardine and Michael Silverthorne is highly interpretive.

I am deeply indebted to Prof. James C. Morrison of St Michael's College, University of Toronto, for introducing me to the importance of Francis Bacon in our modern world, as well as to Prof. Robert K. Faulkner, my dissertation advisor at Boston College, a wise and judicious scholar.

I am grateful to Timothy Burns at *Interpretation: A Journal of Political Philosophy* for permission to draw heavily from my 1994 article "Bacon's *New Atlantis*: The Christian Hope and the Modern Hope," as well as to the good people at Catholic University Press for generous use of my 2010 chapter "Civil

Religion as Political Technology in Bacon's *New Atlantis*," in Weed and von Heyking's *Civil Religion in Political Thought*.

I thank Discovery Institute's Center for Science and Culture for generously funding my participation in the 2018 C. S. Lewis Fellows Program. Thanks to Nathan Shannon for agreeing to include Francis Bacon in the Great Thinkers series and allowing me to write the volume. Thanks to The King's College for the generous supply of books they funded for my study in writing this book. Joshua Hershey, my colleague, not only reviewed my manuscript, but did so with joy and enthusiasm at a busy time of year—because that's who he is. Thanks to A. Edward Major for his consultations on the details of ancient English law and government, to my faculty assistants, Aidan Gauthier and Edward Wilson, for their work in proofreading, to my wife, Jessica, for her suggestions for greater readability, and to my son David and my daughter Eowyn, who supplied me with coffee, refills, and Sous Vide Egg Bites at our local Starbucks as I wrote without distraction.

INTRODUCTION

Why should a thoughtful, modern reader care about Francis Bacon (1561–1626)? The most pressing reason is that we live in Bacon's world. He planned it all, and we participate unwittingly in his grand project. The American pragmatist John Dewey wrote, "Francis Bacon of the Elizabethan Age is the great forerunner of the spirit of modern life . . . the real founder of modern thought."[1] "Modern man," writes Howard White, one of Bacon's most sober interpreters, "is essentially a Baconian."[2] In studying Francis Bacon, we are studying what makes the modern world and us as modern people modern. It is, therefore, an exercise in genealogical research, autobiographical reflection, and intellectual and spiritual self-assessment.

Bacon is arguably the father of modern science, but perhaps the reader is not interested in science. In our modern world, however, science touches everything, shapes everything, tells

1. John Dewey, *Reconstruction in Philosophy* (1920; repr., Boston: Beacon, 1948), 28.
2. Howard B. White, *Peace among the Willows: The Political Philosophy of Francis Bacon* (The Hague: Martinus Nijhoff, 1968), 10.

everything what it is and what it may aspire to become. Science is no longer just a part of life, but has become the whole of life— as Bacon claimed it ought to be. It is widely accepted in our day, and has been for some time, that to know something as true, one must have the facts, data, measurable and quantifiable observations, and these analyzed scientifically. This is scientism, the exclusivity of natural science as a way of knowing. It is premised on philosophical naturalism and is a form of radical empiricism, materialism, and what Auguste Comte later formulated as positivism. It is what Bacon has bequeathed to us, and we embrace it religiously.

The focus of this book is where Bacon himself placed it: his central project and grand ambition for our conquest of nature. He called this his Great Instauration, "a total reconstruction (*instauratio*) of sciences, arts, and all human knowledge, raised upon the proper foundations" (*GI* 66), so that "there may spring helps to man, and a line and race of inventions that may in some degree subdue and overcome the necessities and miseries of humanity" (*GI* 80). This is, he said, "the real business and fortunes of the human race" (*GI* 84). Great hopes for the future were opening up during the Renaissance, inspired by advances in learning, exploration, prosperity, and invention. These inventions were, to be sure, few and haphazard, but they stirred interest in a widening sphere of human possibilities. It took Francis Bacon, however, to show the way to discover nature's closely guarded secrets and, applying them, to open the way for "whole troops of works."[3]

These inventions and works are what we now call technology. Technology is not just cool things that make life better: easier, safer, more efficient, more exciting. Technology, technological thinking, and technological culture are inseparable from each

---

3. *GI* 81; cf. *NO* I.70, 121.

other and give us both the spirit of innovation and the religion of human autonomy, forward-looking hope, and backward-looking suspicion and disdain. Technological culture prefers the novel just for its novelty, is always pushing some envelope and proud to be shattering preconceived notions. This is "the spirit of modern life" of which Bacon was the architect and apostle.

But this project was a hard thing "to win faith and credit for" (*GI* 67). People's hope was in Christ, his resurrection, and his eschatological kingdom, which, at the very least, considerably relieved the urgency of Bacon's "kingdom of man, founded on the sciences" (*NO* I.68). It was part of his plan, therefore, to adapt Christianity as a vehicle for his new scientific civilization. Bacon's project certainly seems Christian, and Bacon presents it that way, as simply an investigation of God's works for "the glory of the Creator and the relief of man's estate" (*AL* 147–48). But there are disturbing details that should lead us to question the Christian standing of his project and thus of "the spirit of modern life." He substitutes the hope of technological science for the Christian hope. Bacon promised us a better blessing, an earthly one, a new continent of learning (*GI* 73) that was to be, by the nature of that learning, identical with a happy land of unprecedented comfort and security.

His promise has borne fruit, but like everything under the sun, it combines both felicity and vanity. Were it not for Bacon, there would be no antibiotics, no plastics, and no internet, but there would also be no atom bomb, no strip mining, and no internet. Insofar as Bacon's hope is the systematic fulfillment of the creation mandate, it is a blessing. Insofar as it is simple domination of the world and thus of some people over others, it is a curse. Pursued exclusively on its own terms, there is no reason it should not culminate in Aldous Huxley's World State in *Brave New World* (1936) or in the National Institute for Coordinated Experiments in C. S. Lewis's space trilogy (1938–45). J. B. S.

Haldane, a prominent British evolutionary biologist, Baconian to his bones, whose thought is said to have been the dystopian inspiration for both Huxley and Lewis, celebrated "man's gradual conquest, first of space and time, then of matter as such, then of his own body and of other living beings, and finally the subjugation of the dark and evil elements of his own soul."[4] (How he derived his notions of "dark and evil," light and good, is anyone's guess.) Bacon was aware of the frightening downside, but thought it worth undertaking just the same, if only for his own posthumous glory.

None of this should be taken to suggest invalidating or disparaging experimental science and its industrial application. Insofar as it is good, it is from God, an obedience to his creation mandate and an explication of "the book of his works," as Bacon put it. As such, it must have biblical foundations. But to be established more firmly on those foundations, the original grounds and their presuppositions—even their overtly stated ones—require fresh examination. Bacon is eloquent on these matters, though also at times artfully elusive. But that just makes it fun.

---

4. From *Daedalus, or Science and the Future* (1923), quoted in John G. West, "The Magician's Twin," in *The Magician's Twin: C. S. Lewis on Science, Scientism, and Society*, ed. John G. West (Seattle: Discovery Institute Press, 2012), 30.

ABBREVIATIONS

AL   *The Advancement of Learning*, in *The Major Works*, ed. Brian Vickers (New York: Oxford University Press, 2002)

GI   *The Great Instauration*, in *Selected Philosophical Works*, ed. Rose-Mary Sargent (Indianapolis: Hackett Publishing Company, 1999)

MBT   *The Masculine Birth of Time*, in *The Philosophy of Francis Bacon*, by Benjamin Farrington (Chicago: University of Chicago Press, 1966)

MW   *The Major Works*, ed. Brian Vickers (New York: Oxford University Press, 2002)

NA   *New Atlantis*, in *The Major Works*, ed. Brian Vickers (New York: Oxford University Press, 2002)

NO   *The New Organon*, in *Selected Philosophical Works*, ed. Rose-Mary Sargent (Indianapolis: Hackett Publishing Company, 1999)

TC   *Thoughts and Conclusions*, in *The Philosophy of Francis Bacon*, by Benjamin Farrington (Chicago: University of Chicago Press, 1966)

Works   *The Works of Francis Bacon*, ed. James Spedding, Robert Leslie Ellis, and Douglas Denon Heath (London: Longmans and Co., 1870)

1

BACON'S HEROIC AMBITION

Francis Bacon, by any measure, is one of the "great thinkers" of the human race. These are, by God's grace, the great masters of that uniquely human faculty—the mind—in its relation to comprehending God, man, and the universe.

Not everyone occupied with ideas is engaged in the same enterprise. Many of these in every direction are mere *idea manipulators*—chattering academics, poseurs, and widely read dilettantes who trade in ideas to fill their pockets and chalk their names on walls of honor. Many others, by contrast, whom we may call *idea mediators*, faithfully curate and elaborate the traditions of thought as fruitful fields of study in support of wisely lived lives—truth-driven scholars and faithful, studious teachers and pastors, even learned artists and poets. *Idea masters*, however, are few. They think within a tradition, brilliantly following its trajectory and developing its logical, metaphysical, and moral implications. But fewer still and rare are the *idea monarchs*, great founders of the highest ambition, who recast and govern whole civilizations by an empire of the mind. Francis Bacon—the father of modern science as a rigorous way of understanding all things and of bringing all things under human control—aspired to be, and is, such a ruler. The question whether his government is wise is a matter of contentious debate. It is a debate over modernity itself.

Bacon stated his great and comprehensive ambitions in a letter to his uncle, Lord Burghley, in 1592 at the mature age of 31: "I confess that I have as vast contemplative ends, as I have moderate civil ends: for I have taken all knowledge to be my province." He underscored the centrality of this intellectual preoccupation: "This, whether it be curiosity, or vain-glory, or nature, or (if one take it favourably) *philanthropia*, is so fixed in my mind as it cannot be removed" (*MW* 20). Many years later, in the proemium to *The Great Instauration*, the introduction to his broad project, he restates his purpose: "to commence a total reconstruction of sciences, arts, and all human knowledge, raised upon the proper foundations" (66). By this refounding and rebuilding of our mental universe, Bacon would reorient all human beings to all things, even to God himself. To his uncle, he allowed that his motive in this could be intellectual curiosity, personal vainglory, or just the controlling impulse of a contemplative nature. The reader should note from the start that Bacon was silent on love for God and allowed only for philanthropy as a generous view that one could take of his aim. In his 1605 work, *The Advancement of Learning*, he writes that what we should seek from knowledge and what we should expect from the progress of its advancement is "a rich storehouse for the glory of the Creator and the relief of man's estate" (*AL* 147–48). Although Bacon couples God's glory with man's comfort, the main thrust of his rhetoric is the hope of human betterment, to which he appeals for enlisting the best minds and the broad public in this new orientation to the world.

The World as It Was

It is difficult for us to appreciate, from the cushion of our modern comfort, the precarious condition of daily life that almost everyone suffered for most of human history. This was ·"man's estate" that Bacon had in mind when he announced his comprehensive philosophical project that would bring us "relief." The aged Jacob lamented to Pharaoh in Egypt, "Few and evil have the days of the years of my life been" (Gen. 47:9 KJV). His sojourn was not unusual, and nothing changed for millennia to come. Job noted that we are "few of days and full of trouble" (Job 14:1). No one would dispute the teacher in Ecclesiastes, who wrote, "What has a man from all the toil and striving of heart with which he toils beneath the sun? For all his days are full of sorrow, and his work is a vexation" (Eccl. 2:22–23).

The fourth horseman of the Apocalypse on his ashen steed, bringing sword, famine, and plague, has cut through human society with dread regularity until very recently (Rev. 6:8). These three evils are, of course, interrelated. Famine and war produced conditions that made especially the poor and those crowded into cities susceptible to disease. One can get a telling picture of the brevity, uncertainty, and cruelty of ordinary, pre-modern life by contrasting the Black Death of the fourteenth century (arguably the greatest public health disaster the world has ever seen) and the miseries of the roughly two hundred years following Bacon's life with the twentieth-century advances in human betterment.[1]

1. In my accounts, I rely on Barbara W. Tuchman, *A Distant Mirror: The Calamitous 14th Century* (New York: Ballantine Books, 1978); Tim Blanning, *The Pursuit of Glory: The Five Revolutions That Made Modern Europe: 1648–1815* (New York: Penguin, 2007); Deirdre McCloskey, *Bourgeois Equality: How Ideas, Not Capital or Institutions, Enriched the World* (Chicago: University of Chicago Press, 2016); and Steven Pinker, *Enlightenment Now: The Case for Reason, Science, Humanism, and Progress* (New York: Viking, 2018).

Famine

Historically, most people have spent their time and energy, like birds and squirrels, securing sufficient food to sustain themselves and their families in life. People lived in continual fear of a failed harvest and a consequent famine. Poor growing conditions from either too much or not enough rain, or from blight, meant starvation for many who were already living at or near subsistence. Grains for seed, cattle, and human consumption had to be grown within just a few miles of where people lived, because a wider distribution network was economically unfeasible or technologically impossible.[2]

So famine was a common horror. "In the European Middle Ages a killing famine in the favored south of England came every ten years or so."[3] A famine in France that lasted from 1692 to 1694 claimed 2.8 million people, 15 percent of the population. Famine killed a third of the people in Finland between 1696 and 1697.[4] A Dutch merchant recounted what he witnessed during a famine in India in 1630–31.

> Men abandoned towns and villages and wandered helplessly. It was easy to recognize their condition: eyes sunk deep in the head, lips pale and covered with slime, the skin hard, with the bones showing through, the belly nothing but a pouch hanging down empty. . . . The whole country was covered with corpses lying unburied.[5]

The last killing famine in England was in 1623. On the continent, France and Germany saw their last one in the eighteenth century, and poor Spain suffered Europe's final famine in

2. Blanning, *The Pursuit of Glory*, 50.
3. McCloskey, *Bourgeois Equality*, 23.
4. Blanning, *The Pursuit of Glory*, 52.
5. Quoted in Pinker, *Enlightenment Now*, 69.

1905.[6] Modern shipping and rail opened Europe to the vast productive plains of the New World and helped turn famine into a history lesson. Mechanization from the industrial revolution that began in late eighteenth-century England radically transformed human productivity and well-being. "In the mid-19th century it took twenty-five men a full day to harvest and thresh a ton of grain; today one person operating a combine harvester can do it in six minutes."[7] Industrial-scale fertilizer from nitrogen in 1909 multiplied yields while slashing the cost of produce.[8] Cooler cars of iceberg lettuce made their first cross-country trip in 1919, turning California farms into America's back garden. Norman Borlaug's Green Revolution in the 1960s turned "lands of famine" like India into grain exporters by engineering wheat, corn, and rice to produce many times more on the same acre of land. In 1947, half the world was malnourished, with consequences for sickness, education, and prosperity. Today, that figure is 13 percent for the developing world alone. Famine is now isolated in the horn of Africa, and has more to do with bad government than bad climate.[9] That is the edible dimension of the technological revolution, of Bacon's dreams and calculations.

Disease

Malnutrition left people especially susceptible to disease. While deadly disease was common, and plague would visit from time to time, the great plague of biblical proportions was the Black Death of 1347–51. People thought it was the end of the world. Why wouldn't they?

This cloud of death came from the east—India, Crimea, and the Levant—and entered Europe by the ports of Messina

6. McCloskey, *Bourgeois Equality*, 23.
7. Pinker, *Enlightenment Now*, 75.
8. Ibid.
9. Ibid., 78.

and Marseilles. From there it spread from Iceland in the west to Russia in the east. Death was hideous, tortuous, and certain. First came "shivering, vomiting, acute headache and pain in the limbs," followed soon by "strange black swellings about the size of an egg or an apple in the armpits and groin. The swellings oozed blood and pus and were followed by spreading boils and black blotches on the skin from internal bleeding." Along with this, "everything that issued from the body—breath, sweat, blood from the buboes and lungs, bloody urine, and blood-blackened excrement—smelled foul."[10] The contagion was spread by rats and fleas and between humans by contact and breath.

Anywhere from one-third to two-thirds of every major city in Europe fell victim. Half of Paris perished and half of Avignon; Florence lost three- to fourth-fifths and Venice two-thirds. The sick were "dying too fast for the living to bury." Whole villages were emptied, their humble structures then swallowed back into the earth. Fields lay unattended, not only from the death of owner and laborer alike, but from a general despair about the future. Why plough and plant when the only reaper is death?[11]

The seventeenth century, the hundred years following Bacon's call to war on nature, was a public health disaster. Spain's population fell from 8.5 to 7 million, devastated by bubonic plague, typhus, and smallpox. The Great Plague of London in 1665 killed up to 100,000 of the 500,000 residents. Naples lost half its population in 1656, and Genoa 60 percent.[12] The eighteenth century was no better. It was part of the rhythm of life for a host of diseases to cut through the population from the least to the greatest: influenza, typhus, dysentery, scarlet fever. But "the great killer of the eighteenth century," Blanning tells us, "was smallpox," which in Europe killed roughly 400,000 people

10. Blanning, *The Pursuit of Glory*, 58; Tuchman, *A Distant Mirror*, 92.
11. Tuchman, *A Distant Mirror*, 94–95, 99.
12. Blanning, *The Pursuit of Glory*, 57, 59.

per year.[13] In the twentieth century, it killed 300 million before it was completely eradicated in 1977.[14]

Of course, there was medicine in and around Bacon's time, but it was based largely on astrology and maintaining a balance among the body's four humors: blood, black bile, yellow or red bile, and phlegm. A physician would restore health by draining off one or another of these by various purgatives or by bleeding, hence the common use of leeches to treat maladies.[15] Tuchman notes that "medicine was the one aspect of Medieval life, perhaps because of its links with the Arabs, not shaped by Christian doctrine." Even highly respected papal physicians based their diagnoses and prescriptions partly on the movement of the sun, moon, and planets. In 1348, the University of Paris medical faculty located the cause of the Black Death in "a triple conjunction of Saturn, Jupiter, and Mars in the 40th degree of Aquarius" in 1345, a judgment that was universally accepted among the learned.[16]

They had no idea of epidemiology. The living would carry out the dead, dwell amongst their piled, stinking corpses, and wear their discarded clothes. The bubonic plague was thought to be spread by beams of light darting from the eyes.[17] Folk remedies for common ailments and diseases were far more likely to help than anything from the medical art, which was likely only to make things worse. So Bacon remarked, "Empirics and old women are more happy many times in their cures than learned physicians" (*AL* 213), and Thomas Hobbes, we are told, "was wont to say, that he had rather have the advice, or take Physique from an experienced old Woman, that had been at many sick

13. Ibid., 62–63.
14. Pinker, *Enlightenment Now*, 64–65.
15. Blanning, *The Pursuit of Glory*, 66.
16. Tuchman, *A Distant Mirror*, 102–3.
17. Ibid., 102.

people's Bedsides, then from the learnedest but unexperienced Physitian."[18]

It follows that sanitation was appalling. In the century of Bacon's birth, people of the lower sort crowded into cities, uncomprehending in their filth and in close society with rats, lice, and fleas. "Before the 20th century, cities were piled high in excrement, their rivers and lakes viscous with waste, and their residents drinking and washing their clothes in putrid brown liquid."[19] Where people congregated

> was a habitat of . . . narrow, airless, filth-ridden streets and passages; of hovels and grand houses without ventilation; of the dead incompletely isolated from the living. . . . We must pause for a moment to try to recapture these scenes . . . of refuse and waste strewn here and there that filled the eyes of the seventeenth-century European.[20]

It is a wonder that anyone survived.

Indeed, historically, average life expectancy has been consistently low, hovering until recently around thirty years of age. There were old people, of course. The Bible refers to a life span as threescore and ten. But high infant mortality rates dragged the average down precipitously. After that, life's usual predators—famine, disease, and war—took their toll.

But much changed when the Baconian view of nature and of reason's purpose in dissecting, measuring, and conquering nature became broadly accepted and rigorously applied. We hit what Dierdre McCloskey calls "the blade of the hockey stick," a period

---

18. John Aubrey, *Brief Lives*, ed. John Buchanan-Brown (London: Penguin, 2000), 442.

19. Pinker, *Enlightenment Now*, 63.

20. James Riley, *The Eighteenth-Century Campaign to Avoid Disease* (New York: Palgrave Macmillan, 1987), x–xi, quoted in part in Blanning, *The Pursuit of Glory*, 59.

of astonishing worldwide improvement in the conditions of life that she calls "the Great Enrichment."[21] Steven Pinker reports that "a British baby who had survived the hazardous first year of life would have lived to 47 in 1845, 57 in 1905, 72 in 1955, and 81 in 2011." Today, having conquered diseases like polio and smallpox, and having introduced antibiotics, antisepsis, pest control, vaccination, chlorinated water, industrial fertilizer, and crop rotation, global life expectancy—global, mind you!—is 71.[22] Winston Churchill reflected on the astonishing pace of progress in "the fuller life of man" that science had generated.

> In the methods of production and communication, in the modes of getting food and exchanging goods, there was less change between the time of Sargon and the time of Louis XIV than there has been between the accession of Queen Victoria and the present day. Darius could probably send a message from Susa to Sardis faster than Philip II could transmit an order from Madrid to Brussels. Sir Robert Peel, summoned in 1841 from Rome to form a government in London, took the same time as the Emperor Vespasian when he had to hasten to his province of Britain. The bathrooms of the palaces of Minos were superior to those of Versailles. A priest from Thebes would probably have felt more at home at the Council of Trent two thousand years after Thebes had vanished than Sir Isaac Newton at a modern undergraduate physical society, or George Stephenson in the Institute of Electrical Engineers. The changes have been so sudden and so gigantic that no period in history can be compared with the last century.[23]

This is all precisely what Bacon foresaw for his project.

21. McCloskey, *Bourgeois Equality*, 24.
22. Pinker, *Enlightenment Now*, 59, 53.
23. Winston S. Churchill, "Fifty Years Hence," in *Thoughts and Adventures* (1932; repr., New York: W. W. Norton, 1991), 193, 195.

Bacon's Plan to Change the World

In the beginning, God gave his human creatures his creation mandate to be fruitful, multiply, fill the earth, and exercise dominion over all things in his name, in his service and for his glory, executing his will out of love for him (Gen. 1:26–28). For this task, we were incapacitated by sin in the fall. Our service became self-seeking. Our rule became rebellion. Efforts at dominion became willful domination—not creative vice-regency, but usurpation and tyranny.[24] Nonetheless, our capacity for unfolding the possibilities within the creation remained—hence, the long history of many inventions in building, plumbing, textiles, agriculture, cookery, warfare, and so on.

After our fall into sin, God told Adam and Eve, "By the sweat of your face you shall eat bread" (Gen. 3:19). Paul tells us that the creation is "groaning," and that the ultimate relief from suffering and death will come with the consummation of Christ's redemption, at which time, and not before, there will be "no more death, nor sorrow, nor crying" (Rev. 21:4 NKJV). Yet, until then, his mercy is upon and throughout his creation. He makes the sun to shine on the just and the unjust alike. His goodness is not only in what we effortlessly receive, but also in what we cultivate from the creation as received, even for the wicked after the fall. We see this in the early chapters of Genesis, specifically in the children of Cain: the invention of agriculture, viticulture, metallurgy, music, poetry, and cities. God does this, not only out of his mercy and as a testimony to his gracious goodness, but also out of love for his people who benefit from these mercies.

Despite these mercies, pestilence and poverty haunted us like

24. For an expanded treatment of this point, see David C. Innes *Christ and the Kingdoms of Men: Foundation of Political Life*, chapter 1, "The Kingdom of God: The Theological Framework for Political Life" (Phillipsburg, NJ: P&R Publishing, 2019); 1–20.

merciless, devouring wolves. Life under the sun was unpredictable, fraught with dangers and difficulties, even for those who toiled faithfully in righteousness. The Preacher reflects: "I saw that under the sun the race is not to the swift, nor the battle to the strong, nor bread to the wise, nor riches to the intelligent, nor favor to those with knowledge, but time and chance happen to them all" (Eccl. 9:11). But with the success of his project, Bacon promised us relief from toil and the uncertainty of life.

Bacon states his plan for alleviating the miseries of our human condition in *The Great Instauration*,[25] the name he also gave to the project he presented in various works, some of which were never published. The heart of the plan is in the work's proemium: the conquest of nature for the empire of man over the universe. He opens with these words:

> Being convinced that the human intellect makes its own difficulties, not using the true helps which are at man's disposal soberly and judiciously, whence it follows manifold ignorance of things, and by reason of that ignorance, innumerable mischiefs. (66)

In stating the problem, that "the human intellect makes its own difficulties," Bacon is saying nothing new. The human intellect has problems: the noetic effects of the fall, the effect of sin on the mind. For this reason, we have lost Adam's original ability to understand the creation. The wise are few, and there is little agreement on anything, even among the learned. Bacon tells us that the reason for these difficulties is not the irremediable nature of things, however, but the inexcusable sloth and negligence of the

25. Charles Whitney points out that the Vulgate Bible, Jerome's translation of the Bible from the original Hebrew and Greek into Latin, uses *instauratio* to indicate restoration as well as a new beginning (*Francis Bacon and Modernity* [New Haven: Yale University Press, 1986], 23).

mind itself—inexcusable because the true helps (by which he means the scientific method outlined in his writings) are at hand.

Bacon then states what he means by intellectual difficulties: the "ignorance of things" that results directly from this neglect of the proper method of inquiry, which in turn brings upon us *rerum detrimenta innumera*, "countless harmful things." The difficulties are not for the mind only, but for the whole wretched human condition. Bacon accounts for these inexhaustible *rerum detrimenta*, or human miseries in general, by our ignorance of "things" perpetuated through this negligence. The remedy is humanly available and near at hand. Bacon's proposal for a new science will right all that is wrong, or at least alleviate the misery.

The traditional Christian teaching on the cause of human misery, however, even regarding the mind alone, is that it stems from the fallen character, not only of man, but of the whole creation. Human misery and the troublesome relationship of man to the rest of creation, whether intellectually or otherwise, is fundamentally but not exclusively a spiritual problem. The remedy must, therefore, be ultimately spiritual, and it is provided in the redemptive work of Jesus Christ. We have the God-given ability to improve our condition—everything from the toil of ploughing and harvesting to the mastery of Jubal's lyre—but every attempt to ground happiness in human works is vain and idolatrous.

Yet Bacon identifies the broadest conception of our difficulties—"innumerable"—as stemming, not from human sin, but from the "ignorance of things." Our ignorance, he says, is specifically regarding the internal operation of things, ignorance that results from "not using the true helps which are at man's disposal," namely his new organon, the new logic and method of discovery. Stated otherwise, the human problem is not theological sin, but philosophical sin, proceeding from ignorance, rather than spiritual rebellion. Thus, all our hopes turn on the relationship, not between the soul and God, but between the mind and "things."

Our salvation from the bondage of misery is found in the restoration of this relationship "to its perfect and original condition,
or if that may not be, yet reduced to a better condition." Although
Bacon adds this qualifier so as not to appear to advocate attempting to reverse Adam's curse or to remedy by human efforts the
consequences of the fall, he has not made a direct, pious statement, as he could have made, but an impious statement followed
by a pious correction.[26] The qualification "if that may not be"
leaves open the possibility that the first, more extreme statement
could be true. The helps that Bacon's method will supply will
restore to the mind the "true powers" God intended for it. But
this requires a revolution in "the entire fabric of human reason,"
the very process of human thought itself, with a view to discovering truth. As the foundation is wrong, so too is everything we
build upon it. Our whole way of thinking about nature is poorly
constructed and must be rebuilt from the ground up. This will
deliver us from life's "innumerable mischiefs," the many ills that
beset the human race, even those for the resolution of which people have traditionally looked to God.

This project, he says, is a hard thing "to win faith and credit
for" (*GI 67*), but it is "that one path which alone is open to the
human mind." He elaborates:

> And certainly the two ways of contemplation are much like
> those two ways of action, so much celebrated, in this; that the
> one, arduous and difficult in the beginning, leads out at last
> into the open country, while the other, seeming at first sight
> easy and free from obstruction, leads to pathless and precipi-
> tous places.

26. This is preceded by a similar impiety, which is, in turn, followed by a pious
correction, namely that there is nothing on earth that compares to the commerce
between the mind and things in this regard, or at least nothing "that is of the earth,"
pulling back from slighting the ministry of Christ's church, for example.

Here he invokes the familiar gospel teaching regarding the two ways:

> Enter by the narrow gate. For the gate is wide and the way is easy that leads to destruction, and those who enter by it are many. For the gate is narrow and the way is hard that leads to life, and those who find it are few. (Matt. 7:13–14)

But in the Sermon on the Mount, Jesus is not speaking of action alone, but of whole ways of life and the principles by which one orders one's life. He is speaking comprehensively. So too is Bacon. Though appearing to distinguish contemplation from action, theory from practice, he actually undermines the distinction. In *Thoughts and Conclusions*, he compares empirics to ants, which merely "gather and combine," and rationalists to spiders, which contribute solely from within themselves. As a model for philosophy, Bacon prefers the bee, which combines the two (*TC* 97). In this metaphor, reason cannot grasp eternal truths or guiding moral principles, but is solely production-oriented. This subordination of thinking to action is not limited to the realm of natural science. This new method or way of contemplation, "a better plan," constitutes "a total reconstruction of sciences, arts, and all human knowledge, raised upon the proper foundations" (*GI* 66). The new method of scientific inquiry is in fact a new logic for understanding everything and thus has revolutionary implications for how we think about, understand, and thus live every aspect of human life.

With the announcement of his project, "the great instauration of the dominion of man over the universe,"[27] Lord Verulam brings good news of great hope. If Jesus is the true path in the

---

27. This is how Bacon characterized his project in the subtitle to an early work, *The Masculine Birth of Time*.

Gospel according Matthew, this new science, Bacon intimates, is the world's true savior. While Jesus says, "I am the way, and the truth, and the life" (John 14:6), Bacon says of his method, "There are and can be only two ways of searching into and discovering truth. . . . This is the true way, but as yet untried" (*NO* I.19).

2

BACON'S COMPLEX CHARACTER

His Life: Bacon's Twin Peaks

Sir Francis Bacon, England's Lord Chancellor and the father of modern science, was a man of broad interests—literary, legal, political, historical, and philosophical—ambiguous personal character, and masterful but measured speech. This has made him difficult to understand without great care and caution. Accordingly, scholars from across the academic disciplines have been divided over what to make of him and his disparate ambitions.

In 1561, in London, little Francis made his blessed entry into the world. He was the younger of two sons born to Sir Nicholas Bacon, the Lord Keeper of the Great Seal under Queen Elizabeth I, by Anne, the daughter of Sir Anthony Cooke, who was tutor to King Edward VI. His mother was a deeply devoted Calvinist and studied in Latin, Italian, French, and Greek. She provided the celebrated translation from the Latin for John Jewel's 1564 *Apology in Defence of the Anglican Church*, a significant work in the religiously unsettled Elizabethan era. His father,

Sir Nicholas, was a man of high standing in Elizabeth's government, second in power only to the Lord Treasurer, William Cecil,
Lord Burghley, who was Francis's uncle. His father and his uncle
were the so-called "two pillars" of Elizabeth's government. Bacon's
extraordinary intellect was evident from an early age. At age
twelve, when he was first introduced to Elizabeth, Her Majesty
was "much taken" with the gracious wit with which he reported
his age: "Two years younger than Your Majesty's happy reign."
With his natural gifts, the classical and Christian education from
his mother, and his privileged access to the royal court, Francis
Bacon was positioned to become as close to a philosopher king
as Plato could reasonably have imagined.

Bacon was educated at Trinity College, Cambridge, between
July 1573 and December 1575. It was the custom to attend university at age fourteen, but as Francis was precocious and close
to his brother Anthony, elder by two years and also attending
Cambridge, he began at twelve. He was drilled in the Greek and
Roman classics and the logic of Aristotle, for which he developed an early distaste. He found the learning of his day, for which
Aristotle was the unquestioned authority, beset with what he
later called "contentions and barking disputations."[1] The rest of
his intellectual life was spent elaborating on the deficiencies of
the received logic and on the "dignity and proficiency" of a new
one. After three years in Europe with England's ambassador to
France for instruction in matters of state and for education more
broadly, he returned to England upon news of his father's death.
He was just eighteen years of age.

Sir Nicholas died quite prematurely of a chill. He had
gathered lands for all his children in the event of his passing,
but was still working on providing for his youngest, Francis.
"Environment and education had bred in him the greatest

---

1. *GI* 69; cf. *AL* 141.

ambitions, but had left him without means."[2] So he began his legal studies at Gray's Inn and was admitted to the bar as an utter (i.e., junior) barrister in 1582 and then as a bencher, able to argue cases at Westminster, in 1586.

He was elected to Parliament for the first time in 1581, and represented various constituencies over the length of his public career. Political life kept him quite busy. He urged the execution of Mary, Queen of Scots (1586), served on a committee to review existing statutes (1588), advised the queen in private correspondence on foreign and domestic affairs (1584) and on managing disruptions from Puritan and Catholic factions (1589), was made a Queen's Counsel in 1596, and, under James, served as a commissioner for Union with Scotland. During this time, he first circulated and then published a handful of essays that culminated in the first edition of his *Essays, Civil and Moral* (1597).

In 1591, he sought to advance his interests by attaching himself to the Earl of Essex, from whom he received considerable favors. But Essex was a soldier of reckless ambition and was executed in 1601 for leading a rebellion against Elizabeth. After the Earl's capture, Bacon was appointed to lead an investigation into the matter. It was awkward to be positioned between friend and sovereign, both of whom deserved his loyalty, or, in the case of Essex, at least not his enthusiastic prosecution. But the rebel's associates were hanged along with him, and Bacon had reason to believe he might have joined them as the price of moral courage.

Two years later, after Elizabeth's death in 1603, James ascended to the throne and Bacon was knighted. At this time, he began publishing his great intellectual ambitions, which he fully expected would define his life for ages onward, as indeed they did. He produced various Latin works, including *The Masculine Birth*

---

2. J. G. Crowther, *Francis Bacon: The First Statesman of Science* (London: Cresset, 1960), 155.

of Time in which he declares, "I am come in very truth leading to you Nature with all her children to bind her to your service and make her your slave." This subjugation, he promises, "will over- come the immeasurable helplessness and poverty of the human race" and "make you peaceful, happy, prosperous, and secure" (*MBT* 62, 72). This was no sudden turn of mind. Eleven years earlier, in an appeal to Lord Burghley for support, he confessed to "have taken all knowledge to be my province" (*MW* 20). But these works were only preparatory to his first great work, this time in English, *The Advancement of Learning*, in 1605. The years 1603 to 1609 were productive years for Bacon in formulating and organizing his thoughts in various writings, the substance of which would make its way into *The Great Instauration*, which he published along with *The New Organon* in 1620.

At age forty-five, just before his years of rapid political ascent from 1607 to 1618, he married. He most certainly had not "fallen in love." For Bacon, everything was a calculation of personal advantage. He begins Essay No. 8, "Of Marriage and Single Life," declaring, "He that hath wife and children hath given hostages to fortune; for they are impediments to great enterprises, either of virtue or mischief." What Tolkien said of Saruman could justly be said of Bacon: "He has a mind of *metal and wheels.*"[3] Alice Barnham was the almost fourteen-year-old daughter of a wealthy London merchant and alderman. Bacon began wedding negotia- tions when she was eleven.[4]

He was appointed Solicitor General in 1607 and Attorney General in 1613. He joined the King's Privy Council in 1616 and became Lord Keeper, like his father, the following year. Finally, he was given the title Lord Chancellor in 1618, one that his father had humbly declined. Honors ensued. That same year, he was

3. J. R. R. Tolkien, *The Two Towers* (New York: Ballantine Books, 1965), 96.

4. Lisa Jardine and Alan Stewart, *Hostage to Fortune: The Troubled Life of Francis Bacon* (New York: Hill and Wang, 1999), 289–90.

created Baron of Verulam, and in 1621, Viscount of St. Albans. Then came the fall.

Just three years after surpassing his father in glory, he was convicted of receiving bribes, "a crime very unbecoming a philosopher," Voltaire later quipped.[5] Because officeholder salaries were low, it was not unusual for a public official to accept gifts. But Bacon had enemies. Although the king allowed him to retain his titles and remitted the enormous fine of £40,000, and Bacon served only a few days of his sentence to the Tower of London, he was exiled from the halls of power.

He retired to write at Gorhambury, his country home since he was a boy. But he continued to claw and beg for power and standing. Nonetheless, these final years were tremendously productive intellectually. His writings included a Latin translation of *The Advancement of Learning* in 1623, *New Atlantis* in 1624, and the third and final edition of his *Essays*. He died in 1626 after complications from an impromptu experiment in refrigeration involving, according to Thomas Hobbes, stuffing a chicken with snow on a roadside.[6]

◆ ◆ ◆

We still ask Lytton Strachey's question, "Who has ever explained Francis Bacon?"[7] and there is much to explain. Perez Zagorin summarized the puzzle this way: "Francis Bacon lived two separate but interconnected lives."[8] One was the contemplative life of Christendom's sharpest, most capacious and eloquent mind, a mind of vast intellectual ambition. The other was the interminably

5. Voltaire, *Letters concerning the English Nation*, ed. Nicholas Cronk (Oxford: Oxford University Press, 1999), 50.

6. John Aubrey, *Brief Lives*, ed. John Buchanan-Brown (London: Penguin, 2000), 29–30. Jardine and Stewart dispute these circumstances in *Hostage to Fortune*, 502–5.

7. Lytton Strachey, *Elizabeth and Essex: A Tragic History* (New York: Harcourt Brace, 1928), 9.

8. Perez Zagorin, *Francis Bacon* (Princeton: Princeton University Press, 1998), 3.

active public life of a political climber, a Machiavellian opportunist, alternately aggrandizing and abasing himself.

Upon his father's sudden death, many suggested that Bacon solve his financial difficulties by practicing law, a profession for which he trained at Gray's Inn. But he refused. He could have sought an academic position, but that would not have satisfied him. He desired political office. "His heart and affection," writes Rawley, his secretary, "was more carried after the affairs and places of [state]."[9] Although he combined both scientist and politician in his soul, he was fundamentally a man of politics.

On the political side of Bacon's life and character, the puzzle has two aspects. On the one hand, Zagorin tells us that Bacon's political ambitions

> absorbed a large part of his time and energy, pitting himself against rivals in a continual competition for office and power, diverting him from pursuing some of his most cherished intellectual goals, and forcing him to leave his main philosophical enterprise fragmentary and unfinished.[10]

This unceasing quest for ever higher political office raises the question: why would someone so committed to benefiting the human race through a radical reorientation of the intellect, as Bacon claimed he was, pursue high office so obsessively for the whole of his adult life? While public service is honorable and requires people of ability and integrity for it to be done well, many others were qualified for that task, whereas Bacon alone had the insight and learning required for "the great instauration of man over the universe."

Bacon justified his tireless pursuit of political power by the

9. *Works* I.6.
10. Zagorin, *Francis Bacon,* 3.

ability it would give him to support coordinated, publicly useful, scientific inquiry with the requisite human and financial
resources.[11] He had in mind something like the National Science
Foundation, or, better yet, Salomon's House as he describes
it in *New Atlantis*. Thus, Bacon reconciled his two seemingly
incompatible and personally consuming goals, the scientific and
the political, by interpreting the political enterprise in terms of
the scientific. But there is no evidence that Bacon ever used his
power to give significant support to the work of science as he
was planning it out.

Bacon's explanation is unconvincing, especially coming from
a man who calculated his actions as carefully as he did. The like-
lihood of his success in achieving a sufficiently powerful position
in government, holding it long enough, then using it successfully to arrange the cooperation of whoever was necessary for the
advance of his great project was uncertain at best, unpromising
at worst. As it turned out, he did not become Lord Chancellor
until 1618 at the age of fifty-seven, just three years before his
downfall and eight years before his death, neither of which he
could foresee. For a life plan, it would have been an un-Baconian
reliance on fortune.

Given his extraordinary learning and eloquence, it would have
been a more efficient use of Bacon's time, with a more promising
outcome, if he had pursued his projects from a position of academic and literary prominence and used his powerful persuasive
abilities to enlist the great in his cause. But Bacon had no interest
in a life so far removed from the direct exercise of political power
and the enjoyment of its honors. Even after he was deposed from
office, instead of turning his full attention to writing and publishing for a more lasting legacy, he continued to lobby for power,
even if only for the right to take his seat in the House of Lords.

11. Ibid., 57–58.

The second aspect of the puzzle of Bacon's politics is the great difficulty he had in accomplishing his goals. Given his connections, education, and extraordinary abilities, he should have danced his way to success. But he was frequently passed over, and rose to the ranks he did only by constantly (as he lamented near the end of his life) "asserviling" himself.[12] People generally saw through his deceits and were repelled by them, earning him distrust rather than influence. Bacon often cited Machiavelli with great admiration, but lacked the *virtu* that successful Machiavellianism requires. He was a notorious manager of his own image for political purposes. In doing so, he prudently concealed himself. "I had rather know than be known," he wrote.[13] Zagorin, a sympathetic writer, observes, "In his personal relationships with the great and powerful whose favor he desired, his preferred methods were dissimulation, subservience, and flattery." In relationships generally, "he regarded other persons purely as means he could exploit to attain his ends. His object was to aggrandize himself by craft, flattery, and displaying himself in the best possible light."[14] Like an orphan, radically alone and vulnerable in a hostile world, Bacon saw only rivals and instruments. In Essay No. 48, "Of Followers and Friends," the only mention he makes of friends is at the end of the essay, where he writes, "There is little friendship in the world," and what friendship there is, "is between superior and inferior, whose fortunes may comprehend the one the other." All friends are followers, useful for advancement.

Bacon lived, in fact, three mutually incompatible lives. Whereas his political life compromised his philosophical life, his sexual life compromised his political fortunes. Puritan Parliamentarian and diarist Simonds D'Ewes recorded what was commonly known: "Yet would he not relinquish the practice of

12. Ibid., 9.
13. *Promus of Formularies and Elegancies*, in *Works* XIV:13.
14. Zagorin, *Francis Bacon*, 14, 20.

his most horrible and secret sin of sodomy . . . nor did ever that I could hear forbear his old custom of making his servants his bedfellows."[15] Aubrey cites Sir Anthony Weldon writing that he was a pederast.[16] His mother and brother speak openly of his male "bed companions" in their letters to him.[17] Perhaps this is why, as Jardine notes, "Bacon was never a good judge of the men in his life," hitching his star to the disastrous Essex, a man he should have seen was incapable of the moderation and dissimulation that Bacon advised. If Bacon wanted the safest path to high office, then—like Elizabeth, his queen—he should have prudently committed himself to chastity.

These contradictions are puzzling only if one accepts Bacon as a genuine philosophical philanthropist with an inscrutable political fixation. His life makes more sense, however, if we interpret his scientific project in light of his political ambitions, that is, his highest political ambition. He did, after all, express his philosophical project in strikingly political language: science is about "the conquest of nature" and "the kingdom of man."[18] William Harvey, best known for his later discovery of the circulation of blood, observed, derisively, that Bacon "writes philosophy like a Lord Chancellor."[19]

Bacon expresses his thoughts on ambition in *The New Organon* (I.129). He first states that there are two grades of honors, one for benefiting one's country and the other for benefiting the human race. Shortly afterwards, he describes three grades of ambition: for oneself, for one's country, and for the human race.

15. Quoted in Jardine and Stewart, *Hostage to Fortune*, 464.
16. Aubrey, *Brief Lives*, 29.
17. Zagorin, *Francis Bacon*, 12; Jardine and Stewart, *Hostage to Fortune*, 103.
18. Tom van Malssen argues that Bacon was fundamentally a political philosopher, that he had an overall project, and that all his works fit into a grand political project and must be understood in light of that. See especially *The Political Philosophy of Francis Bacon* (Albany, NY: SUNY Press, 2015), chap. 2, "The Baconian Turn."
19. Quoted in Aubrey, *Brief Lives*, 143.

Only the latter two correspond to levels of honor because no one honors someone who benefits merely himself. He has received his reward. We honor those who give themselves for others. This allows for the possibility, however, that someone might benefit his country or the human race out of ambition for himself.

But there are honors that surpass even these. Authors of inventions, he says, are divinely honored, regarded by later generations not merely as heroes but as gods. While the benefits to one's people are for only a few ages, discoveries available to mankind last forever. But if an inventor is divinely honored for his great benefits to the human race, how much greater honor, Bacon asks, should the inventor of the means of invention receive? Of course, this superlatively divine honor can belong to only one man: Francis Bacon. It is interesting to note that Thomas Jefferson regarded Bacon, Newton, and Locke as "the three greatest men the world ever produced," calling them his "trinity."[20] In saying this, he was not unusual in his day.

Francis Bacon was a man of soaring personal ambition and equally high personal capacities, the sort of person who could naturally benefit the human race, as indeed he did. But he allowed himself to be distracted from his highest goals and most lasting glories by lesser and incompatible accomplishments and pleasures. It is not unheard of, from Xenophon to Kuyper, to combine the active and contemplative lives, and Bacon was fully aware of their complex relationship. In 1603, he wrote in an unpublished work, "It is hard to say, whether mixture of contemplations with an active life, or retiring wholly to contemplations, do disable and hinder the mind more."[21] His movement among the great of England in such extraordinary times no doubt informed his

20. Letter to John Trumbull, Feb. 15, 1789, and letter to Dr. Benjamin Rush, Jan. 16, 1811, in Thomas Jefferson, *Writings* (New York: Library of America, 1984), 939, 1236.

21. *Valerius Terminus: Of the Interpretation of Nature*, in *Works* III.252.

reflections on human affairs. But that is not why he gave himself professionally to alliance-building, cunning intrigue, groveling and flattery, pomp and vanity, and, of course, matters of law.

If the philosopher is, as Plato says, the one who leaves the cave to pursue the truth, and who would rather remain above, disengaged from the city's concerns, especially its daily concerns, to enjoy the contemplative life without distraction, then, despite his reputation, Bacon was no philosopher. He was obsessed with the cave and could not even enjoy a graceful retirement in devoted writing and study. His philosophical reforms were to give us control of the cave and Bacon himself glory among the cave-dwellers. Yet, his high political ambitions and his philosophical goals were, as he pursued them, in tension with one another. Both were practical. Both were also political. His political goals were not transpolitically oriented, that is, driven by truths that transcend political circumstances, because his philosophical goals were not genuinely philosophical. For this reason, though celebrated for centuries for delivering on his promise of human power over nature, Bacon ultimately failed philosophically as much as philanthropically. We see this in the continuing debate over the goodness of the Baconian modernity of our modern world.

His Reputation: Bacon's Tides of Glory

The inscription on the monument at St. Michael's Church, St. Albans, to Francis Bacon, Baron of Verulam, Viscount St. Alban, adds titles more suited to his glory: *Scientiarum Lumen, Facundiae Lex,* "the light of learning, the law of eloquence." The irony is that, if his body had instead been thrown down a well, his name would be honored nonetheless by the monuments of his books and their fruits.

For much of the twentieth century, it was commonplace to dismiss or belittle Bacon's role as the father of modern science, saying that his method was insufficiently mathematical or that it simply bore little resemblance to what science had become.[22] Alexandre Koyré, a French philosopher of science, called it "a bad joke" to suggest that Bacon had anything to do with the scientific revolution.[23] Yet, for more than 250 years, the greatest philosophers and men of science alike held him in the highest esteem in that role.

Barely two generations after Bacon's death, in his dedicatory poem for Sprat's *History of the Royal Society of London* (1667), Abraham Crowley compared Bacon to the prophet Moses:

> Bacon at last, a mighty man, arose
> Whom a wise king, and Nature, chose
> Lord Chancellor of both their Laws.
> Bacon, like Moses, led us forth at last,
> The barren Wilderness he past,
> Did on the very Border stand,
> Of the blest Promise'd Land
> And from the Mountain top of his Exalted Wit,
> Saw it himself, and shewed us it.

Writing in 1697, John Locke paid tribute to Bacon's intellectual authority to overturn the logic of the ages, calling him "the great Lord Verulam."[24]

In the eighteenth century, no less than Jean-Jacques Rousseau called him "the greatest perhaps of philosophers," who, along with René Descartes and Isaac Newton, was one of the

---

22. For a survey of views, see Robert K. Faulkner, *Francis Bacon and the Project of Progress* (Lanham, MD: Rowman & Littlefield, 1993), 8–11; Rose-Mary Sargent, "General Introduction," in *Selected Philosophical Works*, ed. Rose-Mary Sargent (Indianapolis: Hackett, 1999), xxxii–xxxiv.

23. Zagorin, *Francis Bacon*, 260.

24. John Locke, *Of the Conduct of the Understanding* (published posthumously in 1706), sect. I, "Introduction."

"preceptors of the human race."[25] Thomas Jefferson commissioned a portrait of Bacon to hang alongside those of Newton and Locke in his State Department office. He told the American painter John Trumbull, "I consider them as the three greatest men that have ever lived, without any exception, and as having laid the foundation of those superstructures which have been raised in the Physical and Moral sciences."[26] Benjamin Franklin, himself a noteworthy man of science, considered Bacon "justly esteem'd the father of the modern experimental philosophy."[27]

In the nineteenth century, William Whewell was one of the most learned and intellectually influential people of his time, Master of Trinity College, Cambridge, from 1841 to 1866, and a fellow of the Royal Society. His views on the history and philosophy of science carried enormous weight. He coined the term *scientist*. This man called Bacon "the supreme Legislator of the modern Republic of Science."[28] Charles Darwin tells us in his *Autobiography*, "I worked upon the true principles of Baconian induction."[29] Neil Postman, an especially astute student of modernity, called Bacon "the first man of the technocratic age," as it was he who, though he "was not himself a scientist" and "did not uncover any new law of nature or generate a single fresh hypothesis," nonetheless "first saw, pure and serene, the connection between science and the improvement of the human condition."[30]

25. Jean-Jacques Rousseau, *Discourse on the Sciences and Arts*, in *The First and Second Discourses*, ed. Roger D. Masters (New York: St Martin's, 1964), 62–63.

26. Letter to John Trumbull, February 15, 1789, in Jefferson, *Writings*, 939.

27. Benjamin Franklin, *Poor Richard's Almanack*, in *Writings* (New York: Library of America, 1987), 1252.

28. See Markku Peltonen, ed., *The Cambridge Companion to Bacon* (Cambridge: Cambridge University Press, 1996), 1.

29. Charles Darwin, *The Autobiography of Charles Darwin*, ed. Nora Barlow (New York: Norton, 1969), 119.

30. Neil Postman, *Technopoly: The Surrender of Culture to Technology* (New York: Vintage, 1993), 35–36.

The twentieth-century disparagement of the technical adequacy of his method misses Bacon's most profound accomplishment: reorienting our stance toward the universe and inspiring our hope in its conquest. To understand Bacon as simply the progenitor of "science" as a particular academic discipline or class of disciplines would be to misunderstand both Bacon's ambitions and his profound effects. Bacon saw himself as a man of practical ambitions that were as wide as the world, but who nonetheless took, as he said, "all knowledge to be my province" (*MW* 20). His goal was nothing short of changing the way human beings reason about everything with the goal of bringing everything in the universe under human control for whatever we choose to do with it—relief, convenience, but inevitably the power and glory of a few.[31]

Some are even more contrarian in denying the scientific revolution altogether, claiming instead a continuity between medieval and modern science.[32] The science of the Christian Middle Ages, they argue, was highly productive and provided the foundation for the science we so treasure today for its bountiful blessings. Happily, the characterization of medieval European history as "the Dark Ages," an age "lit only by fire," has been amply refuted.[33] With all due respect to the riches of the

31. For surveys of Bacon's reception historically, see Faulkner, *Francis Bacon and the Project of Progress*, chap. 1, "A Plan and Its Interpreters"; Sargent, "General Introduction," in *Selected Philosophical Works*.

32. Stanley Jaki, *The Road of Science and the Ways to God* (Chicago: University of Chicago Press, 1978); Edward Grant, *The Foundations of Modern Science in the Middle Ages* (New York: Cambridge University Press, 1996), and *God and Reason in the Middle Ages* (Cambridge: Cambridge University Press, 2001); Rodney Stark, *For the Glory of God: How Monotheism Led to Reformation, Science, Witch-Hunts, and the End of Slavery* (Princeton: Princeton University Press, 2003).

33. The term "Dark Ages" originated with Italian Renaissance scholar Francesco Petrarch (1304–74). For the narrative that depicts this period, even the culturally vibrant Late Middle Ages, as one of universal ignorance and superstition, so widely accepted today as a truism, see Edward Gibbon, *The History of the Decline and Fall*

medieval Christian world in theology, philosophy, architecture, and the arts, especially following the Crusades and the rediscovery of Aristotle in the twelfth and thirteenth centuries, it would be a gross equivocation and serious error to suggest that what was termed natural philosophy in the European Middle Ages could claim any paternity for what we now call science. This was Bacon's argument, and men of science for the next 250 years agreed with him. The critical and most consequential difference is that medievals made no attempt to discover the inner principles of nature (*NO* I.99).

Arguments for continuity often focus on medieval inventions. The three commonly cited are gunpowder, the printing press, and the magnetic compass, but historians of science also mention spectacles, windmills, flying buttresses, and stirrups. These were based, however, on scant and careless observation, came from no understanding of natural principles, and had no connection with the scholars of the medieval university.[34] Even Leonardo DaVinci (1452–1519), so marvelously productive in inventions, left us no method, no guidance for natural inquiry. Bacon contended that though there were impressive inventions that had transformed warfare, navigation, and the

---

of the Roman Empire, vol. 6 (1788), chap. 37; Henry Thomas Buckle, *The History of Civilization in England* (1857); Jacob Burckhardt, *The Civilization of the Renaissance in Italy* (1860); J. W. Draper, *History of the Conflict between Religion and Science* (1874); Andrew Dickson White, *A History of the Warfare of Science with Theology in Christendom* (1896). Two recent books that have, with great prejudice, sustained this view in the popular mind are Daniel Boorstin, *The Discoverers* (New York: Random House, 1983), and William Manchester, *A World Lit Only by Fire* (New York: Little, Brown, 1993).

34. Consider Lynn White, *Medieval Technology and Social Change* (Oxford: Oxford University Press, 1962), and Stark, *For the Glory of God*, 128–34. Stark cites saddles and harnesses as medieval "technologies" (132). But though products of the *techne* of the mechanical arts, they had no relation to the *logos* of science. For a deeper, more sophisticated understanding of these inventions and their emergence from and place within medieval society, see Postman, *Technopoly*, 22–29.

dissemination of knowledge, they were ad hoc and came by accident, driven by practical necessity. Instead, he showed the way to a steady and ever swelling flow of inventions, fed by the light of nature.

In current accounts of the scientific revolution, we hear of Copernicus, Galileo, and Kepler, whereas Bacon, who invented nothing and himself made no discoveries, is passed over as a mere popularizer of what grew out of the Late Medieval and Renaissance intellectual soil. "Historians have long since debunked Bacon's old reputation as the father of modern science," writes Charles Whitney, "and ironically some have moved toward reducing his stature to that of prophet in the sense of cheerleader, advance man, or, precisely, trumpeter."[35] But he brought together, perfected, and gave force to what had been developing for a couple of centuries. That goes far beyond being a mere "popularizer."

Many of Bacon's criticisms of the medieval, bookish approach to science and his great esteem for the practical over the merely theoretical were circulating among artisans and men of practical inquiry in the generations leading up to his own. Paolo Rossi, a great scholar of the Late Renaissance and of Francis Bacon in particular, notes that "Bacon brought to full awareness some of the thematic ideas that had been making slow headway at the margins of the official science in that world of technicians, engineers, and builders."[36] Late Medieval Europeans were not people of democratic views: there were noble and vulgar classes. Accordingly, some activities and objects of study were viewed as beneath the dignity of gentlemen. The aristocracy considered the mechanical arts base, a form of servile labor.

35. Charles Whitney, *Francis Bacon and Modernity* (New Haven: Yale University Press, 1986), 4–5.

36. Paolo Rossi, *Philosophy, Technology, and the Arts in the Early Modern Era*, trans. Salvator Attanasio (New York: Harper & Row, 1970), 117–18.

Rossi notices a pattern of concern among artisans and philosophers between 1530 and 1580 that "men of culture must give up their contempt for 'operations' or 'practice' and discard every conception of knowledge that is merely rhetorical or contemplative to turn to the observation and study of techniques and the arts."[37] But the cultural battle that necessarily preceded the wide embrace of productive science was far from won. Bacon fought it to his dying day because victory for scientific civilization required the help of his genius. In 1680, half a century after Bacon's departure, Richelet's *Dictionnaire Français*, in its article on "Méchanique," reads, "This term, speaking of particular arts, signifies that which is the opposite of liberal and honorable; it has the connotation of baseness and of being little worthy of an honest person." Much later still, Rossi tells us, "the French Jesuits were scandalized by what they thought was an excessive number of articles on technical subjects in Diderot's *Encyclopédie*."[38]

Robert Norman, an English sailor who manufactured magnetic compasses and wrote on magnetism, was already, in 1581, attacking the Western philosophic tradition for its indifference to the practical fruit of inventions. Like many of his day, he expected far more of learning than the ancients and their followers could deliver. But like these others, he saw only some of the problem, and, accordingly, only some of the solution. As early as 1603, Bacon called for a new "commerce between the mind and things" for there to be any great progress in multiplying inventions. But he was not the first. Bernard Palissy, a distinguished French potter (notice: practical, base), claimed in 1580 that the art of observing nature must be founded on a "cult of things," as opposed to bookish learning and philosophical speculation.[39] Bacon, however, had far more in mind than Palissy, a potter, ever could.

37. Ibid., 10–11.
38. Ibid., 12.
39. Ibid., 5, 2.

While the mechanic had been able to gain some insight into the workings of nature and had produced useful works, this field of activity was not the answer to the miserable condition of mankind. In *The New Organon*, Bacon points us beyond this type of labor. "The study of nature with a view to works is engaged in by the mechanic, the mathematician, the physician, the alchemist, and the magician, but by all (as things now are) with slight endeavor and scanty success" (I.5). By giving priority to "experiments of light" that patiently investigate nature's inner workings (and do so by the instrument of a suitable method) rather than grasping prematurely at applications, Bacon promises to "supply practice with its instruments, not one by one, but in clusters, and draw after them trains and troops of works" (*NO* I.70).

Markku Peltonen, editor of *The Cambridge Companion to Bacon*, reports that in the latter twentieth century, Francis Bacon's "importance in early modern philosophy has been restored. His plan of scientific reform has been given a central place in historical accounts of the birth of the new science." But even this falls far short of appreciating Bacon's lofty goals and grand accomplishment. Bacon's corpus is no aggregate of random writings that expressed the unrelated interests of a Renaissance man. Peltonen holds the view that "philosophy, though clearly important to Bacon, was only one facet of his life."[40] But Bacon's high claims for this "facet" indicate that philosophy, as he conceived it, was far more comprehensive in scope. He saw his intellectual project as a unified whole—the Great Instauration. The *Essays* prepare the minds of people and reorient them. The great nineteenth-century British historian Thomas Babington Macaulay remarks, "It is in the Essays alone that the mind of Bacon is brought into immediate contact with the minds of ordinary readers."[41] Bacon refutes

40. Peltonen, ed., *Cambridge Companion to Bacon*, 1–2, 10.
41. Thomas Babington, Lord Macaulay, "Lord Bacon," in *Critical and Historical Essays*, 5th ed., vol. 2 (London: Longman, Brown, Green, and Longmans, 1848), 426.

the old learning and argues for the new in *The Advancement of Learning*, and presents the new method of reason in *The New Organon*. *New Atlantis*, published after his death (which, mind you, he did not expect to come so soon), presents an inspiring vision of the scientific society that awaits us at the end of "the true way" of discovery that is "as yet untried" (*NO* I.19).

The status of Bacon's thought and his legacy in the twenty-first century stand or fall with this project, his design for it, its character, and its necessary consequences.

His Religion: Bacon's Dubious Faith

Bacon is remembered as a pious man, inspired by charity and guided by Holy Scripture. Thomas Fowler, for example, a prominent nineteenth-century Bacon scholar, calls Bacon's faith "robust," writing that "he sought God in nature, and there he recognized, reverenced, and adored Him."[42] Benjamin Farrington, an Oxford interpreter, pictures Bacon as a religiously motivated man, a man of prayer, who sought for the human race only what he found that Scripture testifies is theirs, namely "dominion over all creatures."[43] Bacon left much support in his writings for the view that his intentions and the reformation in learning for which he strove were godly.

Many writers accept Bacon's religious pronouncements *prima facie*, but there is reason to probe them. Bacon had cause to dissemble on this matter. It was unacceptable to be outwardly irreligious at that time. This was especially true for someone of high political ambition. And if one was proposing a way of thinking about the world that would transform our view of everything,

42. Thomas Fowler, ed. *Bacon's Novum Organum*, 2nd ed. (Oxford: Clarendon Press, 1889), 50, 53.
43. Benjamin Farrington, *Francis Bacon, Philosopher of Industrial Science* (London: Lawrence and Wishart, 1951), 4–5.

it would have been wise to persuade a Christian civilization that one's innovation was fully in harmony with the reigning faith. Dissembling on points of religion would have been all the more advisable if that project was already an object of godly suspicion. For this reason, some read Bacon more circumspectly and make a more observant assessment of his piety.[44]

In fact, godly seventeenth-century readers were highly skeptical of Bacon's enterprise. It smacked of pride and avarice, of the atheistic and materialistic atomism of Democritus, and of the Epicureanism of Lucretius. Bacon wrote works like *The Advancement of Learning* to defend his project against these charges, against "the zeal and jealousy of divines" (122). The fictional *New Atlantis* was to show—in response to doubters—how knowledge of nature's depths could actually support the work of charity and the glory of God. Bacon also taught the necessity of dissembling, of deception and prudent concealment, and was adept at it—showing oneself at half lights and mixing a lie with the truth,[45] the better to gain welcome where otherwise one's ideas would be refused.

Bacon understood what T. S. Eliot wrote concerning the subtle power of poetry, and he practiced it consciously and effectively in his own rhetoric. "The chief use of the 'meaning' of a poem, in the ordinary sense, may be . . . to satisfy one habit of the reader, to keep his mind diverted and quiet, while the poem does its work

44. Faulkner, *Francis Bacon and the Project of Progress*; David C. Innes, "Bacon's *New Atlantis*: The Christian Hope and the Modern Hope," *Interpretation* 22, 1 (1994): 3–37, and "Civil Religion as Political Technology in Bacon's *New Atlantis*," in *Civil Religion in Political Thought*, ed. Ronald Weed and John von Heyking (Washington: Catholic University of America Press, 2010); Timothy Paterson, "On the Role of Christianity in the Political Philosophy of Francis Bacon," *Polity* 19, no. 3 (1987): 419–42; Jerry Weinberger, *Science, Faith, and Politics* (Ithaca, NY: Cornell University Press, 1985); Howard B. White, *Peace among the Willows: The Political Philosophy of Francis Bacon* (The Hague: Martinus Nijhoff, 1968).

45. Essay No. 1, "Of Truth," and Essay No. 6, "Of Simulation and Dissimulation."

upon him: much as the imaginary burglar is always provided with a nice piece of meat for the house-dog."[46] Eliot compares the poet to the burglar, sneaking into a home with disarming treats for those charged with guarding it against despoiling or destructive intruders. Bacon's religious rhetoric plays the same role. But Bacon is less a thief than a cuckoo. He came not to steal and kill, but to occupy and displace. Lesslie Newbigin used this cuckoo image to describe "the domestication of Christianity within European culture," precisely what Bacon and his philosophical successors sought to achieve in preparing conditions suitable for modern betterment.

> The cuckoo's egg was, as happens in nature, mistakenly supposed by the original owner of the nest, to be one of her own young with whom there could be a happy family life. She had yet to learn that the cuckoo would claim the whole nest. To use a different sort of language, there was the illusion that the meta-narrative of the Gospel and the meta-narrative of the Enlightenment could be fused into a single story of the march of Christian civilization.[47]

Bacon's plan was never merely to supply what was wanting in the Christian world, but to reconstruct that world "upon the proper foundations," assigning "to faith that which is faith's," which is, at best, the role of supportive civil religion and, at worst, private, harmless irrelevancy.[48]

Stephen A. McKnight illustrates this eagerness to believe every pious pronouncement Bacon utters. In *The Religious*

---

46. T. S. Eliot, *The Use of Poetry and the Use of Criticism* (Cambridge, MA: Harvard University Press, 1933), 151.

47. Paul Weston, ed., *Lesslie Newbigin: Missionary Theologian: A Reader* (Grand Rapids: Eerdmans, 2006), 249.

48. *GI* 66, 74; *NO* I.65.

Foundations of Francis Bacon's Thought, he shows only that Bacon's works are awash with religious imagery. Of Bacon's use of the imagery, he is entirely uncritical. What is its role in the success of his project with a Christian and skeptical people? Is the theology he appears to espouse compatible with the philosophy he champions? Does he noticeably contradict himself? Bacon was brilliant, and his works were carefully crafted. If you can see a problem, be assured that he could see it too.

McKnight's book demonstrates how useful it is to be orthodox in one's own understanding of the Christian faith—even with Elizabethan era, Anglican theology as a standard—in assessing Bacon's religious language. As evidence of Bacon's piety, he offers that "Bacon links the instauration of knowledge to the restoration of humanity to its prelapsarian state."[49] He seems unaware of the spiritual audacity of this ambition, as though substituting the hope of Bacon's new method of discovery for the cross, the resurrection, and the new creation were something a Christian might reasonably suggest. McKnight is equally undisturbed in his claim that Bacon relies not only on biblical themes, but also on "the *prisca theologia*, a highly elastic collection of Neo-platonism, Hermeticism, alchemy, magic, and Jewish esoteric traditions."[50] Never mind how unlikely this is for a genius who resolved to "admit nothing but on the faith of eyes, or at least of careful and severe examination" (*GI* 82).

Perez Zagorin also notes Bacon's dream "of reversing the consequences of original sin and restoring humanity through the power of science to its pristine condition before the Fall." He also sees that "the Christian view of the Fall was inconsistent with Bacon's belief in the limitless possibilities opened to

49. Stephen A. McKnight, *The Religious Foundations of Francis Bacon's Thought* (Columbia: University of Missouri Press, 2006), 8, 42, 64, 153.
50. Ibid., 3.

mankind by science, which lay at the heart of his philosophy."[51] Despite this observation, he claims that scholars like Howard White and Robert Faulkner, who caution against an unguarded acceptance of Bacon's pious self-presentation, fail "to produce any evidence or proof to support the claim of Bacon's irreligion." In all of Bacon's writings, he objects, there is "no clue or statements to substantiate this view."[52] Yet, Zagorin himself provides a wealth of it. In those writings, he finds "secrecy, esoteric communication, and the techniques of managing people." Bacon's preferred methods for influencing people were "dissimulation, subservience, and flattery."[53] He provides a two-page account of Bacon's esoteric method of writing, the craft of using the same text to present yourself in one way to one readership—the vulgar and the dangerous—while disclosing your controversial, heretical, or revolutionary thoughts to others, as it were, between the lines, as with artful self-contradiction, the strategic repetition and placement of significant words, brandishing orthodoxies in only superficially convincing ways, and the use of obviously bad arguments in favor of positions you disfavor or against positions you support. He gives multiple examples of Bacon explaining how and why he practices these deceptions.[54]

Substantively, Zagorin says that Bacon wanted to reverse the consequences of the fall and that the heart of Bacon's philosophy is at odds with fundamental Christian belief. He notes that Bacon's own mother had serious doubts about her son's spiritual condition and religious commitment. In writings that Bacon authored exclusively for himself, Zagorin found political ambition and cunning designs, wherein "he regarded other persons purely

51. Zagorin, *Francis Bacon*, 45, 242n60.
52. Ibid., 243n75.
53. Ibid., 14. See also Arthur M. Melzer, *Philosophy between the Lines: The Lost History of Esoteric Writing* (Chicago: University of Chicago Press, 2014).
54. Ibid., 43–44.

as means he could exploit to attain his own ends." He adds, "His object was to aggrandize himself by craft, flattery, and displaying himself in the best possible light." That often involved insincere expressions of religious devotion, especially when one's great innovation on which hung one's everlasting fame sat uncomfortably with or stood in hostile opposition to, the accepted religion. Nonetheless, Zagorin holds, "As for Bacon's personal religion, I have found no reason to question the sincerity of his Christian professions."[55]

Some will cite the testimony of William Rawley, Bacon's chaplain: "This Lord was religious."[56] But Rawley had just told the reader that Bacon was parsimonious in his self-revelation. He observed his Lord Verulam to be a politic man in his conversation with others. His private thought "he vented with great caution and circumspection."[57] Did he share his honest religious beliefs with his chaplain? Or is his faithful chaplain as cautious as he himself was on this point, keeping trust with an eye on his lord's immortal memory, and thus also his own?

What exactly does the chaplain say?

> This Lord was religious: for though the world be apt to suspect and prejudice great wits and politics to have somewhat of the atheist, yet he was conversant with God, as appeareth by several passages throughout the whole current of his writings. Otherwise, he should have crossed his own principles, which were, *That a little philosophy maketh men apt to forget God, as attributing too much to second causes; but depth of philosophy bringeth a man back to God again.* Now I am sure there is no man that will deny him, or account otherwise of him but to have him been a

55. Ibid., 46, 12, 50.
56. William Rawley, *The Life of the Right Honourable Francis Bacon,* in *Works* I:51–52.
57. Ibid., 47.

deep philosopher. And not only so; but he was able *to render a reason of the hope that was in him,* which that writing of his of the *Confession of the Faith* doth abundantly testify.

Rawley directs our attention to Bacon's writings to prove Bacon's piety, though it is his writings themselves that arouse suspicions over the questionable relationship between his innovations and the Christian faith. The argument that Rawley cites from the *Essays* only illustrates Bacon's ambiguity. In that passage, Bacon explains why a little philosophy might lead to atheism, namely, an overemphasis on secondary causes. But he is silent on how deeper philosophical inquiry would reconcile the apparent explanatory sufficiency of these discoveries with the teachings of the faith.

Rawley's argument appeals to the reader's confidence that Bacon would not knowingly contradict himself, that is, lie. But what does Bacon himself say about truth telling? In Essay No. 1, "Of Truth," we read that a "mixture of falsehood is like alloy in coin of gold and silver; which may make the metal work the better, but it embaseth it." In other words, a little falsehood is a useful thing. In Essay No. 6, "Of Simulation and Dissimulation," he says that simulation (open lying) is not immoral or sinful, but only impolitic or imprudent, "except it be in great and rare matters." Habitual lying comes from a weak character and will lead to one's undoing. Dishonesty is not the best policy. But the skillful use of a lie can be of great advantage at appropriate times. Concerning dissimulation, he says, "it followeth many times upon secrecy by a necessity; so that he that will be secret must be a dissembler in some degree." Bacon was quite willing to "cross his own principles" when a politic presentation of himself demanded it. Rawley's choice of arguments indicates that he knows this.

As for the hope that Bacon held in his heart, his *Confession of the Faith* "abundantly testifies" only to Bacon's crafted ambiguity, since he invented a method of science that, as he states repeatedly, gave the human race a powerful, rival hope. That Rawley even addresses the question of Bacon's Christian standing indicates that, even in his own day, Bacon's religious sincerity was suspect.

The spiritual state of Bacon's heart while he lived and when he passed from this world to the next is not our concern. The Christian character of his project, its compatibility with Christian civilization, its corrosive or edifying consequences, and how it can be wisely handled, curtailed, and adapted for godly appropriation in the future, if possible—these are the questions for a student of Francis Bacon who is eager to live wisely in the world.

3

THE PROMISE OF
BACON'S PROJECT

Hope as Method: The New Reason

Bacon titles his work on the scientific method *Novum Organum*, or *The New Organon*, positioning it in opposition to Aristotle's six books on logic known as *The Organon*. The Latin word *organum* means simply "tool" or "instrument." Aristotle's logical works were grouped, therefore, as the tools of learning. Thus, in *The New Organon*, Bacon presents his method of inquiry into nature as the new instrument of learning, the new logic-for-truth. Accordingly, at the end of his dedicatory letter in *The Great Instauration*, he tells King James I: so that philosophy and the sciences will not "float in air, but rest on the solid foundation of experience of every kind," he has "provided the instrument" (*organum*) for the stuff that must be gathered from "the things themselves" (*rebus ipsis*). The principles and procedures he will describe in *The New Organon* are, he tells his king, "quite new, totally new in their very kind."

Critique of the Old Science

As previously noted, there is much trumpeting in some circles about medieval science, its discoveries and inventions, and about the roots of the new science in the old, as though all talk about a "scientific revolution" were just an ignorant modern prejudice.[1] But, as Bacon saw it, what understanding of nature had emerged from the medieval university was "a mere hodgepodge and a heap derived from much credulity [*fide*, faith] and much accident" (*NO* I.97, my translation), mere "coastings along the shore" (*AL* 201). Thus, he says, he will "sweep away all theories and common notions" and commence "a fresh examination of particulars" (*NO* I.97).

In his preface to *The Great Instauration*, Bacon states his objection, as he frequently does, to the inadequacy of the old way of inquiring into nature. The existing sciences

> stand almost at a stay, without receiving any augmentations worthy of the human race, insomuch as many times not only what was asserted once is asserted still, but what was a question once is a question still, and instead of being resolved by discussion is only fixed and fed; and all the tradition and succession of schools is still a succession of masters and scholars, not of inventors and those who bring to further perfection the things invented. (*GI* 69)

Edward Grant describes the role of the *questio* at the heart of the method of medieval science:

---

1. See Edward Grant, *The Foundations of Modern Science in the Middle Ages* (Cambridge: Cambridge University Press, 1996); David C. Lindberg, *The Beginnings of Western Science*, 2nd ed. (Chicago: University of Chicago Press, 2007); Rodney Stark, *For the Glory of God: How Monotheism Led to Reformation, Science, Witch-Hunts, and the End of Slavery* (Princeton: Princeton University Press, 2003).

Hundreds of questions drawn from Aristotle's natural books formed the basis of natural science in the medieval university. To a considerable extent, doing medieval scholastic science meant analyzing and evaluating these questions to arrive at the most satisfactory conclusions. . . . By its very nature, the *questio* form encouraged differences of opinion. It was a good vehicle for dispute and argumentation. Medieval scholastics were trained to dispute and therefore often disagreed among themselves.[2]

Thus, barrenness and futility were the state of the received science. Its end was "to overcome an opponent in argument," rather than "to command nature in action" (77). Hence, those who mastered the science were scholars, not inventors. It was not productive, but polemical. From one age to the next, there was debate and bickering and division into sects, a swirling of opinion, but never any certainty on which to build real accomplishments. Bacon calls this approach to learning "the boyhood of knowledge, and has the characteristic of boys: it can talk, but it cannot generate" (69).

When it did turn its sights to productive work, it was hasty and clumsy. The syllogism, which Bacon identifies as the substance of the received science, is haste elevated to a system of logic. The syllogistic principle is that terms agreeing in a middle term agree thus with each other. For example, Socrates is a man; all men are mortal; therefore, Socrates is mortal. Insofar as this is a point of mathematical certainty, which is what a productive science requires, the syllogism has an appearance of soundness. The problem, Bacon contends, is this: the linchpin, which is the middle term, is completely untrustworthy, being overhastily

---

2. Edward Grant, "Medieval Science and Natural Philosophy," in *Medieval Studies: An Introduction* (Syracuse, NY: Syracuse University Press, 1992), 361.

abstracted from a narrow collection of particulars. The undisciplined inquirer rests only momentarily in experiment, gives only a glance at particulars, and then flies immediately to the most general axioms, deducing from them the intermediate ones. Thus, the natural tendency of the mind to overlook the true nature of things is reinforced by method, not corrected by it. This clumsy investigation is guilty of "letting nature slip out of its hands."[3] Syllogistic reasoning is "properly applied to civil business and to those arts which rest in discourse and opinion," but is "not nearly subtle enough to deal with nature" (72). It is perfectly adequate as logic-for-persuasion, but not as logic-for-truth.

Once it is recognized that the state of the sciences is imperfect, but can be perfected, that is, made adequate to the subtlety of nature, then what can be hoped for in this world through industry becomes theoretically limitless.

Introduction of the New Science

To prepare us for the specifics of induction in Book II of *The New Organon*, Bacon must first, in Book I, change our way of thinking, our way of understanding ourselves, and our orientation to the world. So in the first four aphorisms of *The New Organon*, Bacon states the orienting principles for this transformation. He answers these questions: what can we know and why do we want to know it, or rather, what can we reasonably hope?

The New Organon begins with the word "man" (*homo*) and follows immediately with the word "nature" (*naturae*).

> Man, being the servant and interpreter of Nature, can do and understand so much and so much only as he has observed in fact or in thought of the course of nature. Beyond this he neither knows anything nor can do anything. (*NO* I.1)

---

3. *GI* 77–78; *NO* I.22, 19, 104.

The book's theme is man in his relation to nature. Man, as Bacon presents him here, is not God's image bearer, charged with taking dominion in his name, but "the servant and interpreter of nature." The notion of man as "servant of nature" is an odd one. Though a particular man may be called to serve a particular master or king, mankind is to serve God alone. But only an intemperate reader would draw conclusions based solely on these few words. Nonetheless, the work starts on a suspiciously impious note.

Bacon follows this with a statement concerning the limitations on what men can "do and understand," that is, "so much and so much only as he has observed in fact or in thought of the course of nature." Here Bacon restricts our understanding to what nature reveals. Elsewhere, he distinguishes between nature—the book of God's deeds that reveals his power—and the Holy Scriptures— the book of God's word that reveals his will.[4] Based on this first, straightforward, and unqualified statement, special revelation (the Bible) cannot provide knowledge because it is not "of the course of nature."[5] His use of the word *tantum*, "just so much and no more," indicates that he means what he says when he restricts our understanding, and thus our capacity to act, in this way. So as not to be misunderstood, he restates himself in clearer terms: "Beyond this," that is, beyond what is observed in the course of nature, "he neither knows anything nor can do anything." Bacon does not say "without this." That is, he does not say observation of the course of nature is a prerequisite to any further knowledge based on special revelation. He says "beyond this." Such observation is our exclusive source of knowledge. What Bacon means by "the course of nature" he explains in the third aphorism: "that which in contemplation is as the cause is in operation as the rule." The "course" of nature is the government of cause over effect.

4. *NO* I.89; *AL* 126, 142, 153.
5. Bacon's project, keep in mind, is to refound and reconstruct "all human knowledge" (*GI* 66).

Because of the subtlety of nature, observation cannot proceed simply by naked eyes and the unassisted mind, but requires instruments for the eyes and helps, namely, Bacon's experimental method, for the mind (*NO* I.2). He distinguishes between observation in fact (lit. of "things") and in thought. Observation in fact is experimentation, whereas observation in thought is concluding based solely on that experimentation. In this way, human understanding is limited to the results of methodological investigation into causal relationships. As such, it is cut off in principle from divine revelation.

Having restricted what the mind can know, Bacon then restricts what reason can accomplish, and thus he limits the business that is suitable to reason.

> Human knowledge and human power meet in one; for where the cause is not known the effect cannot be produced. Nature to be commanded must be obeyed; and that which in contemplation is as the cause is in operation as the rule. (*NO* I.3)

Reason's goal is useful knowledge, not moral or metaphysical understanding, which in principle reason cannot reach. "Human knowledge and human power meet in one." Human power, in Bacon's understanding, is the ability to command nature, that is, all of creation. His following statement, "for where the cause is not known the effect cannot be produced," indicates that knowledge is only of causes, which are the keys to the kingdom of nature.

The fourth aphorism follows the same theme of effectual knowledge:

> Toward the effecting of works, all that man can do is to put together or put asunder natural bodies. The rest is done by nature working within. (*NO* I.4)

Both halves of this aphorism pertain to "the effecting of works." It combines our part, which is solely combining and dividing "natural bodies," and "nature working within," which in the first aphorism he called "the course of nature." The combining and sundering makes natural bodies do what they would not do on their own. "The rest" is what Bacon has called obedience to nature (*NO* I.3), allowing natural bodies to do what they would ordinarily do, but under controlled conditions. Think of a chemical compound that results from putting two substances together in a way that would not occur in "nature free and at large" (*GI* 82), and then letting nature take its course.

For Bacon, knowing is strictly for the sake of doing, a distinction that collapses in the third aphorism: "Human knowledge and human power meet in one." Doing and understanding, though separable, are coterminal. Deeds cannot exceed knowledge because "where the cause is not known the effect cannot be produced." Knowledge cannot exceed deeds, not only because deeds alone are the legitimate end of knowledge, but also because knowledge requires deeds as pledges of truth. In *The Advancement of Learning*, Bacon argues that knowledge should "not be as a courtesan, for pleasure and vanity only . . . but as a spouse, for generation, fruit, and comfort" (148). Bacon stated this point more bluntly and most memorably in the more obscure 1597 writing, *Meditationes Sacrae*: "Knowledge is power."[6]

Bacon cautions, however, against a "premature and unseasonable eagerness" for application of discoveries to the comforts of life (*GI* 72). Invoking the myth of Atalanta,[7] he writes, "I do not run off like a child after golden apples, but stake all on the

---

6. *Meditationes Sacrae* No. 11, "De Haeresibus."

7. In the myth of Atalanta, the swift-footed huntress agrees to marry whichever man can outrun her. Hippomenes, being shrewder than he is fast, drops golden apples behind him as he runs, and because Atalanta stops to picked them up, he wins the race and her hand in marriage.

victory of art over nature in the race" (*NO* I.117). He distinguishes between experiments of light and experiments of fruit. Experiments of light aim directly at the principles of nature. They are "of no use in themselves but simply serve to discover causes and axioms" (*NO* I.99). It is on this understanding that he says, "The very contemplation of things as they are, without superstition or imposture, error or confusion, is in itself more worthy than all the fruit of inventions" (*NO* I.129).

Nonetheless, there is no room here for either speculative knowledge or knowledge for the enjoyment and glory of God, for philosophy not directed ultimately to production. The conquest of nature is the sole business of philosophy. Although Bacon elsewhere seems to affirm the value of knowledge simply for its own sake, he concludes with his characteristic pragmatism: "Truth, therefore, and utility are here the very same things; and works themselves are of greater value as pledges of truth than as contributing to the comforts of life" (*NO* I.124).[8] Truth, for Bacon, is like the goose that lays golden eggs. Her value is not in herself, but only as the source of innumerable future eggs.

Bacon uses the first four aphorisms of Book I to cut the reader off from any consideration of divine or metaphysical things. Because these cannot be known by the legitimate method of science—and thus cannot be known—they are unreliable as sources of hope. Bacon prepares his readers for their conversion from heavenly or philosophical devotion to exclusively earthly concerns, and from the Christian hope to the modern, Baconian hope.

The Method of the New Science

The hope that Bacon labors to inspire in us has two aspects. First, the hope-as-goal is the promise of his science, the "Sabbath"

8. Cf. *AL* 167–68.

of rest from our labors and from "the necessities and miseries of humanity" (*GI* 85, 80). Second, the hope-as-method is the power of the new logic, the *novum organum*, the instrument he provides for extracting truth from a guarded and reticent nature. In this instrumental hope, the challenge is in the subtlety of nature and in achieving a subtlety of investigation sufficient to overcome "the difficulties and obscurities of nature" and thus to "command nature in action" (*GI* 77). Each will be considered in its turn.

Bacon understands the subtlety of nature in three aspects: the hidden principles of nature itself, the deceptiveness of the senses, and the troublesome character of the mind. The discoveries of pre-Baconian science "lie close to vulgar notions, scarcely beneath the surface," whereas the method he advocates will "penetrate into the inner and further recesses of nature," where the real business of nature operates (*NO* I.18). Traditional science naively accepts the givenness of the world, nature's candor. It fails to account for what Bacon calls "the subtlety of nature, the hiding places of truth, the obscurity of things, the entanglement of causes, the weakness of the human mind" (*GI* 71). But triumph over nature requires unlocking nature's secrets, "the causes of common things, and the causes of those causes" (*NO* I.119). The foundations of the sciences must be laid here in "the very bowels of nature" (*GI* 79). All other ground is sinking sand. For that reason, method must be employed to compel nature to betray herself.

The unaided senses are wholly inadequate to access this deeper level of reality, which is the most useful for discovery and invention. For this reason, the senses deceive. Nonetheless, "things which strike the sense outweigh things which do not immediately strike it, though they be more important," and thus "the testimony and information of the sense has reference always to man, not to the universe" (*NO* I.50; *GI* 79). Despite his deprecation of sense experience, Bacon is an empiricist because through the helps his method provides, he perfects and enables the senses, accepting what they report only of nature through the discipline of experiments.

If the senses are prone to error, even more so the mind. *The Great Instauration* declares from the start that "the human intellect makes its own difficulties." It does this through what Bacon calls "idols" that possess the mind (*NO* I.38–68). The "Idols of the Tribe" are those "inherent in the very nature of the intellect" (*GI* 80). Although the senses tell lies, the mind makes us desire those lies. Whereas the senses lack the subtlety for penetrating to the root of things, the mind, by its nature, willingly contributes to the distortion and for this reason is more prone to error than the senses. For example, the mind superimposes on the world more order and regularity than actually exists (*NO* I.45). The mind, he says, cannot accept the world as limited, so it invents notions such as teleology, final causality, nature understood as purposive. In this way, he argues, man reads his own nature into that of the universe (*NO* I.48):

> The human understanding is no dry light, but receives an infusion from the will and affections; whence proceed sciences which may be called "sciences as one would." For what a man had rather were true he more readily believes. (*NO* I.49)

The mind's willfulness inclines us toward accounts of the world that follow our preferences instead of the universe itself. For the same reason, the mind has a natural tendency toward useless abstractions that give "a substance and reality to things which are fleeting. But to resolve nature into abstractions is less to our purpose than to dissect her into parts" (*NO* I.51). Thus, while the senses simply report nature's distorted testimony, the mind contributes distortions of its own. If it is to progress in its understanding, the mind must be disciplined "by severe laws and overruling authority," that is, proper method (*NO* I.47).

The true method makes commerce possible between "the mind and things" (*GI* 66). In this sense, it functions as mediator: "the office of the sense shall be only to judge of the experiment, and that the experiment itself shall judge of the thing" (*GI* 79). Bacon compares trying to approach nature with unaided senses to sweeping with only a broom handle. A subtler instrument is needed. Bacon locates the "legitimacy" of his method in its subtlety.[9]

Whereas the received science is hasty in its method and confused in its conclusions, Bacon's is severe in method and certain in results. By severity, he means the sober, strictly disciplined ascent from the particulars themselves to the lowest axioms, and from there to axioms of increasing generality as merited only by the discovery of new particulars, accepting "nothing but on the faith of eyes, or at least of careful and severe examination, so that nothing is exaggerated for wonder's sake" (*GI* 82). The

9. Bacon's use of the word *legitimate* to describe his method calls to mind two converging metaphors—priestly intercession and marriage. A priest is a mediator, marriage requires the mediation of a priest, and both require procedure according to law. As mediator, a priest represents and makes intercession for the people before God. Israel's high priest was specially consecrated to come before God, who was otherwise unapproachable in his holiness by sinful creatures. The priest could serve God and offer acceptable sacrifice only in strict accord with God's ceremonial law. God struck down Nadab and Abihu for offering "unauthorized fire" (Lev. 10:1–3). So too, says Bacon, because of our natural inadequacies and nature's inscrutability, we need a mediator, a priest through whom we approach nature: the experiment itself, or the inductive method. Our deliverance, blessing, and peace come only when nature's laws are observed punctiliously. It is only when science follows nature's hidden laws that there will be commerce or "marriage" between the mind and things. It is only with the priestly ministry of the inductive method that "the bridal chamber of the mind and the universe" may hope to be fruitful with "a line and race of inventions that may in some degree subdue and overcome the necessities and miseries of humanity" (*GI* 80). Furthermore, Bacon, as the father of experimental science, writes of himself, "I perform the office of a true priest of the sense" (*GI* 79). The term Bacon uses for "priest" is not the ecclesiastical *sacerdos*, but the pagan *antistes*. Yet the function this mediator performs is akin to that of a Levitical priest. Whereas the Levitical worship of Israel pointed beyond itself to the high priestly ministry of the Messiah, Bacon points to himself.

resulting understanding will be a true model of the world. When combined with "a due process of exclusion and rejection," the method leads to "an inevitable conclusion" (*GI* 78).

When Bacon says that science aims at discovering the causes of things, he means the discovery of their simple natures or "forms" in his peculiar understanding of the word. Forms are "those laws and determinations of absolute actuality which govern and constitute any simple nature, as heat, light, weight, in every kind of matter and subject that is susceptible to them" (*NO* II.17). They are relatively few in number, and in different combinations explain everything in the universe—thus, their fundamental importance to our hope of commanding nature.

> But whosoever is acquainted with forms embraces the unity of nature in substances the most unlike, and is able therefore to detect and bring to light things never yet done, and such as neither the vicissitudes of nature, nor industry in experimenting, nor accident itself, would ever have brought into act, and which would never have occurred to the thought of man. From the discovery of forms therefore results truth in speculation and freedom in operation. (*NO* II.3)

In other words, it is from the discovery of forms that human beings attain the double end of knowledge and power. As Robert Ellis understands Bacon, a knowledge of forms "would enable us, at least in theory, to solve every problem which the universe can present to us."[10]

Lastly, legitimate experience—lawful evidence—begins with a natural history properly suited to a productive science, so that induction may proceed from particulars themselves. Ancient and medieval science were without certainty and thus barren in part

10. Robert Ellis, "General Preface to Bacon's Philosophical Works," in *Works* I:27.

because they did not provide this "foundation to build philosophy upon." Bacon's natural history is neither for beholding the glorious variety of things nor even for immediate use in experiments, but in due time to produce useful works, "not here and there one, but in clusters" (*GI* 81). Things must be enumerated, methodically investigated, verified, counted, weighed, and measured (*NO* I.98). Nothing can be known that cannot be measured and quantified.

Particulars must be drawn, not only from nature as we find her, "free and at large," but also "under constraint and vexed; that is to say, when by art and the hand of man she is forced out of her natural state, and squeezed and moulded" (*GI* 82). In this way, modern science seeks to penetrate beyond the relatively useless appearances to the unseen causes of things in order to control them for useful purposes. With this, "philosophy and the sciences may no longer float in air, but rest on the solid foundation of experience of every kind, and the same well examined and weighed" (*GI* 68).

Regardless of how closely this method resembles experimental science as currently and most productively practiced, it is not Bacon's precise method that justifies his glory as the father of modern science. Although the method has been modified, the spirit is unchanged. His greatness was and remains ultimately in his reformulation of the purpose of science and all pursuit of knowledge, and thus of our relation to the universe and who we are in that universe. It was not a school that he sought to establish, but the victory of art over nature that is still the business of modern life (*NO* I.117).

Hope as Goal: The New Progress

The modern age is distinguished by its orientation toward, and confidence in, what is called "progress." The sixteenth century, that of Bacon's birth, understood itself quite consciously as modern, as a time of rapid and marvelous change—of advancement in learning and discovery and an explosion of inventions coming out of the Renaissance. Excitement at the idea of unprecedented progress was buzzing among those at the forefront of learning. Tomasso Campanella expressed this in his utopian work, *The City of the Sun* (1602): "Oh, if you knew what our astrologers say of the coming age, and of our age, that it has in it more history within a hundred years than all the world had in four thousand years before, of the wonderful invention of printing and guns and the use of the magnet."[11] But what Campanella saw as a gusher, Bacon saw as a trickle compared to what he knew that properly applied and aided reason could achieve.

Today we take progress for granted. Like gravity and taxation, it's always there. The present is better than the past, and the future will be better than today. Modern science has brought us to this good place, and modern science will carry us forward to better still. That's progress. We understand it primarily in terms of our ever-increasing ability to control the world rather than be controlled by it. That means progressively greater security against the world and one another, and greater comfort in that security. Central to that comfort is choice and command: freedom from constraint in one's choices and godlike command of one's surroundings in robust, perpetual health. "Computer, turn the heat down to 71 and pull up *The Office*, season 3."

This view of life and of life's future is uniquely modern, and it is the frame of mind that Bacon wrote explicitly to inspire in support of his project to remake the world. He sought to accomplish this by changing how we see the world, how we reason about all things: the world, ourselves, good and evil, God and his Word. Crowther notes that Bacon "was the first to propose

11. Paolo Rossi, *Philosophy, Technology, and the Arts in the Early Modern Era*, trans. Salvator Attanasio (New York: Harper & Row, 1970), 65.

the continual improvement of human life by the systematic development and application of science, not as a Utopian dream but as a practical policy."[12] Bacon argued for a hope-driven civilization that organizes itself around the human capacity to take charge of the world, not only for the relief of human suffering, but for "the effecting of all things possible" (*NA* 480). This hope is the promise of the modern scientific enterprise, the confident expectation that by the conquest of nature a particular way of life—one we judge will make us happy—is attainable. It entails a judgment regarding the sort of life that is most attainably satisfying for human beings, and thus entails also a particular theory of human nature and view of God.

It was through biblical religion that hope became a central religious theme and a virtue. Biblical hope is a confident expectation of the highest good. In classical antiquity, hope (Greek: *elpis*) was merely a passion, and thus often misleading. Plato has Timaeus describe hope as "easily led astray."[13] In *Antigone*, the chorus expresses the twofold value of *elpis*:

Wandering hope brings help to many men.
But others she tricks from their giddy loves,
and her quarry knows nothing until he has walked into
    flame.[14]

Because of its foundation in God's revelation, however, biblical hope is not a wish or a "good bet," but a certainty.

The Christian hope is ultimately theological. It begins and

12. J. G. Crowther, *Francis Bacon: The First Statesman of Science* (London: Cresset, 1960), xi.

13. Plato, *Timaeus*, trans. Benjamin Jowett, in *The Collected Dialogues of Plato*, ed. Edith Hamilton and Huntington Cairns (Princeton: Princeton University Press, 1961), 69d.

14. Sophocles, *Antigone*, trans. Elizabeth Wyckoff, in *Sophocles I*, ed. David Grene and Richard Lattimore (Chicago: University of Chicago Press, 1954), 615–19.

ends with God, who is its ground, its means, and its object. It is grounded in the nature of God—immutable, sovereign, and pure—and thereby in the perfect trustworthiness of his word (Titus 1:2–3). The resurrection of Christ secured it historically and testified to its certainty (Rom. 4:24; 1 Cor. 15:20). The Holy Spirit, who indwells the believer, testifies to the same certainty and guarantees its ultimate realization (1 Cor. 2:14; Rom. 5:5; 8:11; 2 Cor. 1:22).

The affecting of this hope is equally Trinitarian. God the Father predestines, calls, justifies, and glorifies his people (Rom. 8:29–30). The Son, by his crucifixion, atones for their sins (Col. 1:20). The Holy Spirit applies this work in the believer (Titus 3:5–7).

Finally, the object or substance of the Christian hope is not the heavenly enjoyment of pleasures that God's faithful, by suffering and toil, were prevented from enjoying in this life. It is God himself in whom the perfected believer, resurrected in body and sanctified in spirit, shall find perfect and eternal satisfaction.

In Bacon's scientific project, hope takes a secular form. In his account of the research activities of Salomon's House in *New Atlantis*, he alludes to what resembles modern accomplishments in, for example, medicine, meteorology, and agricultural science. Bacon himself, however, understands this prescience, not as a passive seeing into the future, but as an active leading through the promotion and establishment of his new science. First by his writings and then by the success of his science, Bacon has been decisive in shaping our own attitude toward the future, which is to say, the character of the hope that animates our civilization.

Whereas *The Great Instauration* argues for the project as a whole and *The New Organon* presents the method for its achievement, *New Atlantis* is a literary presentation of that achievement, a picture of scientific civilization written for the heart. It was a hesitant and skeptical audience for which Bacon wrote this tale.

Men despaired because they believed a science to be impossible that could deliver the power over nature for which Bacon argued. For this reason, *New Atlantis* is not an argument, like *The New Organon*, but a captivating tale intended to inspire hope in a sovereign science that would remedy our woes. The excellence of the science is seen in the allure of Bensalem, his fictional island. Its people are "happy," widely enjoying what is most important to them: the comfort and security produced by a largely triumphant science. Their virtue is their "humanity." This is primarily the disposition to provide others with these goods, the only goods modern science equips us to provide. This virtue also encompasses the toleration and civility underlying the island's religious and civil peace. Bensalem helps us imagine a science-enabled world, a better world—or at least a safer and more comfortable world. The people of Bensalem live peacefully with one another because they give priority to the comforts and security that their science successfully provides.

New Atlantis opens with a picture of premodern, prescientific man, buffeted by the forces of unsympathetic and mysterious nature to which he is wholly subject (457). These men have laid up food for a year. This gathering and rationing is their security against the future. An ugly change in the weather, however, leaves them with nothing. Consequently, the storm of nature, not their own plans, directs their course for months on end. Many of them are also sick, helpless under the power of disease. This is the picture: helpless dependence on circumstances (usually unfavorable) and a life of poverty, making "good spare" of limited resources. In sum, prescientific man is afloat in "the wilderness of waters in the world,"[15] the world unconquered and thus hostile or

---

15. "No holiday-maker sought the sea. It was dangerous, a wreckers' world, unwritten about save in tones of dismay, unpainted save as the background to a miracle or a foreground to the welcoming quays of town" (J. R. Hale, *Renaissance Europe 1480–1520* [London: Fontana-Collins, 1971], 41).

at best indifferent to human needs and desires. Accordingly, the crew "prepared for death," seeing they had no hope.

Just short of despair, Bacon writes, they pray "to God above, who 'showeth his wonders in the deep'" (quoting from Psalm 107:24). In Psalm 107, God, in his loving providence, calms the seas and brings the God-fearing sailors to their desired haven. Jerry Weinberger observes that, in Bacon's parallel account, the winds and seas themselves bring the sailors to a haven they did not foresee and so did not at first desire. Given that we later learn that Bensalem can control the winds and the seas, this suggests that "the providence displayed in the *New Atlantis* replaces the providence of an irresponsible and hostile creator."[16] The sailors' prayer for divine mercy is based on their ignorance of the wonderful power of Bensalemite science. Thus, Bacon signals that, in our mortal struggle against nature, our hope is best placed, not in God, but in the productive science that Bensalem has devotedly undertaken.

With the use of this psalm, Bacon has the sailors turn to God as conceived in a particular way. They cry out not to the God who brought Israel out of Egypt, but specifically to God as he is known through general revelation, as he is revealed in nature. It is only when the travelers look to God so described that they spy "thick clouds" that might conceal a continent or island. At the sight of this, hope stirs within them. Bacon compares his new science, which itself was afar off and shrouded with a thick cloud of uncertainty, to a new continent.[17] Sure enough, the land they discover is the island of Bensalem, the home of Baconian science, the hope of the human race. It is the City of God come down to earth—or at least the city of this god to whom every experiment is a prayer and every discovery an answer to prayer.

16. Jerry Weinberger, "Science and Rule in Bacon's Utopia," *American Political Science Review* 70 (1976): 873.
17. *NO* I.92, 114; cf. *NA* 457.

Comfortable Security

Bacon's use of the word *hope* in *New Atlantis* is in each case associated with preservation of the body. The first occurs in the context of the storm in which the Europeans' ship is tossed. Their hope is the land they sight, their immediate earthly salvation. The second use has reference to preservation against sickness (457, 459). Just as the Christian hope includes the restoration of the body, but spiritual and incorruptible through resurrection in Christ, the Baconian hope is the restoration and preservation of the human body in this world by natural means.[18]

The narrator draws continual attention to how much finer everything is in Bensalem compared to Europe. Bensalemite technology is able to make trees "greater than their nature; and their fruit greater and sweeter and of differing taste, smell, colour, and figure, from their nature" (482). Medical applications are prominent. The travelers are particularly astounded by the seemingly miraculous cures they are provided, such as by Bensalem's scarlet oranges, "an assured remedy for sickness taken at sea" (461). Bacon refers not simply to the curative effects of oranges for scurvy, but to the rapid return of health through techno-oranges.

Their sick "mended so kindly and so fast" that it was as though they were "cast into some divine pool of healing." This remark has two related references. The first is to the pool of Bethesda described in John's gospel (5:1–15). There we see many miserable souls—lame, blind, and in other ways wretched and infirm—waiting for an angel to come down (as on occasion he would) and disturb the waters, bringing healing to whoever was then first to enter the pool. Second, this "divine pool of healing" anticipates the account of the artificial baths that, we are later told, imitate the healing springs found in nature. Among

---

18. Weinberger, "Science and Rule in Bacon's Utopia," 872.

these are employed a certain "Water of Paradise, being, by that we do to it, made very sovereign for health and prolongation of life" (481–82). The divine example looks tightfisted compared to the more humane, technological example. Of course, in the gospel account, Jesus heals the infirm man who is unable ever to reach the pool. Also, the point of the gospel story is the spiritual lesson concerning Christ's messianic identity and his redemptive, restorative grace. In Bacon's view, however, it is the writers of the New Testament who overlook what is important.[19]

Humanity

The travelers are particularly impressed by what they call Bensalem's "humanity," their benevolent disposition to provide for the travelers' needs. Bensalem maintains an institution called the Strangers' House, which caters solely to travelers like these, though it has been thirty-seven years since the last guest (462). Its establishment by Solamona, Bensalem's founder, is said to be a mark of his "humanity" (470). Guests are given "handsome and cheerful chambers," food and drink, "scarlet oranges . . . for sickness taken at sea," and "whitish pills, which they wished our sick should take . . . which (they said) would hasten their recovery." Overwhelmed by these generous provisions, the narrator marvels at their "piety and humanity" (461).

Bacon's use of the term "humanity" in place of "charity" to describe a "Christian" people, however, is telling. Christian charity, or love, is the supernatural work of God in the hearts of the redeemed (1 John 4:7–8). It is ultimately a love for God in Christ and desires above all to direct people to know and love him. Charity is wider in its concern than humanity, comprehending both temporal and eternal benefits while giving priority

19. It is noteworthy that, in 1,900 years of concerted research, Bensalem still has not mastered the techniques of resurrection and perpetual youth. There does not seem, however, to be any reason in principle why these goals should be unattainable.

to the eternal. Charity is uniquely "Christian" in this sense. In *The Great Instauration,* Bacon uses this Christian terminology in addressing his Christian audience. He asks that through his innovations God would "endow the human family with new mercies" as we "cultivate the truth in charity" (74). Bacon's use of the word "charity," like "humanity," indicates only an orientation toward the relief of human misery: the prolongation of life and the wider distribution of innocent worldly comforts and pleasures. In *New Atlantis,* it is because of the "consolations" and "comforts" they receive that the European travelers call Bensalem "a land of angels" (463). Acts of love and humanity can often resemble each other, but to equate them is to truncate love. Yet this is what Bacon does as he reorients the reader's hope from spiritual blessings to earthly benefits.

We also see a transition from the Christian term "mercy" to the secular "humanity." When they were in danger at sea, the Europeans cried out to God for "mercy." The greeting on the scroll offered them "that which belongeth to mercy" (457–58). But the narrator, speaking later as one who has been converted to the ways of Bensalem, describes his hosts as "full of humanity" (458). Just as the European travelers undergo a conversion from the old hope of Christian Europe to the new hope of technological Bensalem, so the reader is carried by rhetorical stages to a new continent of thought. The travelers describe this land of technological marvels as "a picture of our salvation in heaven" (463), but it is a heaven without Christ. Bacon reconditions our understanding of Christian charity to make it useful for the progress of science.

Religious Peace

Though an initial reading of *New Atlantis* gives the impression of a deeply religious writer who would not dream of a future— scientific or otherwise—that was not robustly Christian, careful attention to Bacon's masterful arrangement of details reveals a less comfortable relationship between sincere religion and science pursued in this way. Bacon engineers a subtle shift from the historic Christian faith to a religion that bears sufficient resemblance to it so as not to alarm most readers. But the religion of Bensalem includes significant omissions and departures from what his audience would have considered orthodox.[20] In the preface to *Wisdom of the Ancients*, Bacon explains how to introduce new ideas that are sure to be upsetting: "Even now if any one wish to let new light on any subject into men's minds, and that without offense or harshness, he must still go the same way and call in the aid of similitudes."[21] He draws upon the old religion so as better to establish the new, one better suited to the new world he is attempting to shape.

Bacon's *New Atlantis* seems designed to endear the compatibility of Christianity and modern science to a generation of religious authorities who were skeptical of this new learning. Indeed, it appears as though the coming kingdom of man over nature will make the kingdom of God more fully realizable. There is a sense in which we have seen this. Medical discoveries, as well as inventions in transportation and communication, have extended the breadth and reach of God's mercy and God's word. Modern technology has aided Bible translation and the broadcast of the gospel to "every tribe and language and people and nation" (Rev. 5:9). But that is not the argument Bacon makes. Although the hopes of the new science and of the old gospel appear to be

20. Christian orthodoxy in early seventeenth-century England was measured by the ecumenical creeds and councils, *The Book of Homilies* (1547, 1562, and 1571), and *The Thirty-nine Articles* (1563).

21. *Works*, VI:698. Howard B. White suggests that Bacon has *New Atlantis* in mind with these words (*Peace among the Willows: The Political Philosophy of Francis Bacon* [The Hague: Martinus Nijhoff, 1968], 109). For a thorough account of Bacon's esoteric art of secretive writing, see Van Malssen, *The Political Philosophy of Francis Bacon* (Albany, NY: SUNY Press, 2015), chap. 1, "The Art of Transmission."

compatible, even complementary, the subtle rhetoric of the tale presents the Christian hope as an impediment to the new hope, and thus in need of fundamental alteration.

Bacon shows us orthodox Christianity displaced by a civil religion suited for a new, universally enjoyed human hope of comfort and security—youthful health, longevity, civil and religious peace, "humanity"—in a word, a secular *shalom*. The island's name, Bensalem, means "son of peace" or "epitome of peace." The island's founder and its great research institution are named loosely after Solomon, whose name means "peace." But the peace to which they are dedicated is not peace with God, the peace of hearts that are restless until they rest in him, the peace that passes all understanding. It is a peace on earth based on a subjugation of the earth and limited by our understanding of the earth. This peace is based, not on the reconciliation of man with God, but on the "commerce between the mind of man and the nature of things" (*GI* 66).

Like Europe, Bensalem is a Christian land. The European strangers, who are themselves quite pious, notice the striking religious devotion of the island: "We are come here amongst a Christian people" (461). Upon their arrival, the travelers are asked to swear "by the name of Jesus and his merits" (459). The governor of the Strangers' House is a Christian priest. He is pleased that their first question, concerning the arrival of the gospel there, indicates that they seek first the kingdom of heaven. There was a miraculous revelation of the gospel to the land, followed by a prompt and nearly universal acceptance of it. The Feast of the Family, their major festival, is said to be "a most natural, pious, and reverend custom" (472) and is punctuated with Christian hymns and prayers. The Father of Salomon's House relates the Order's "true state" to the narrator "for the love of God and men." But these features and references serve only to obscure the heterodox character of a religion designed to suit the needs of scientific civilization. Pious Christian displays distract from a more fundamental assault upon, transformation of, and ultimately displacement of, Christianity. It is civil religion.[22]

The reader should notice first that the Europeans view the cross on the scroll as "a certain presage of good" (458), but the connection between this sign and benevolence is not obvious. Back in Europe, Christians are known to kill one another for religious and political reasons. The question the official asks, "Are ye Christians?" is an odd one. His use of the word "Christians," rather than "Catholics" or "Protestants," indicates he is above denominational disputes. Unlike anything that existed in the seventeenth century, his Christianity is ecumenical. It is civil.[23]

Second, the governor of the Strangers' House is, as he says, a Christian priest, but though we see a priest, there are no preachers,[24] and the only priest we meet is unemployed as a priest *per se*. He oversees a ministry of mercy, the Strangers' House, an institution that has not seen work in many years. He takes orders from "the state" (462). Bacon includes a "Christian priest" on his island, but no institutional church to shepherd this ostensibly Christian people. He is said to be reverend, but based on his humanity, not his piety. He says he desires only a priest's reward, which is their brotherly love and the good of their souls

22. For a fuller account of this, see David C. Innes, "Civil Religion as Political Technology in Bacon's *New Atlantis*," in *Civil Religion in Political Thought*, ed. Ronald Weed and John von Heyking (Washington: Catholic University of America Press, 2010).

23. David C. Innes, "Bacon's *New Atlantis*: The Christian Hope and the Modern Hope," *Interpretation* 22, 1 (1994): 15.

24. Bacon was aware of the importance of preaching. He praised the theological insights contained in some of the outstanding sermons of his day: "For I am persuaded, . . . that if the choice and best of those observations upon texts of Scriptures, which have been made dispersedly in Sermons within this your Majesty's island of Britain by the space of these forty years and more . . . had been set down in a continuance, it had been the best work in divinity which had been written since the Apostles' times" (*AL* 297).

and bodies. But we see no evidence of anyone's concern for the soul. The newly arrived travelers are asked whether they are Christians, but only generically. There is no concern for even the broadest orthodoxy. Intense doctrinal concern often destroys the peace that is necessary for the progress of science. But there can be no genuine concern for another's spiritual well-being without at least minimal attention to orthodoxy (1 Tim. 4:16). In Bensalem, the kingdom of God over souls is subordinate to the kingdom of man over nature, if it is given any place at all.

Third, Bacon includes the revelation miracle ostensibly to show, not only that religion in general and Christianity in particular are compatible with his science, but also that they encourage and support one another. The miracle is necessary for the gospel to gain access and acceptance on the island, since Solamona's law forbidding the entrance of strangers predated Christ. Bacon, however, is the author of these details. He chose to introduce that difficulty to show that the new science is independent of Christian revelation and may profitably proceed ungoverned by it.[25]

When the pillar of light and the ark appear miraculously, a curious citizenry approaches them, led by a wise man, or scientist, of Salomon's House. By immediately rowing as near as they can to what they take to be a heavenly sign, they demonstrate a boldness incompatible with belief in a holy God. They ask the Lord "to prosper this great sign, and to give us the interpretation and use of it in mercy; which thou dost in some part secretly promise by sending it unto us" (464). That this miraculous event might be a sign of judgment never crosses their minds. Rather, it is assumed to be "useful," like anything of value, and hence their forwardness in fearlessly approaching this divine spectacle. It may even be said that, to the Bensalemites, God himself

---

25. Weinberger makes a similar point in "Science and Rule," 876n61, 878.

is recognized only insofar as he is useful. For this reason, they understand the Lord only as Creator (464, 471, 488), not as Judge and Redeemer, and his creation solely in terms of utility for comfort and security. The book is replete with examples. In Salomon's House, there are daily hymns and services of praise to God for all his works, except his work of redemption—a glaring omission.

Although the apostle Bartholomew's letter in the ark mentions "salvation," the governor says that it was from "infidelity" that the land was saved. Use of the word *sin*, very common in the seventeenth century, appears to be deliberately avoided. The canonical books and Bartholomew's letter arrive in "a small ark or chest of cedar, dry, and not wet at all with water, though it swam" (465). Bacon repeatedly draws attention away from the letter and the Scriptures, focusing on the ark that transported them. The governor concludes the account, crediting the ark for saving the land from infidelity (not sin and death) as "the old world" was saved from water (not God's judgment).

The ark itself would be of much greater interest to a people of science like the Bensalemites than any nonscientific books it may contain. This ark, though it swims, remains dry. Insofar as it stays dry in the water, it is nature that is overcome or conquered. At the beginning of *New Atlantis*, the seas represent the unknown and unconquerable. The old ark, which in the Bible represents the covenant of grace by which God's people are saved, contrasts with this new ark, which, in its ability to float in the water and yet remain dry, represents the conquest of nature by which all may be saved. It is specifically infidelity to nature from which Bensalem was saved, and this salvation can extend to any land that will faithfully obey nature through the science that commands her. "Nature to be commanded must be obeyed" (*NO* 1.3).

The fourth veil over Bacon's revolutionary religious intentions for scientific society is the Feast of the Family. This celebration, which has the appearance of piety, serves instead radically to undermine the orthodox Christianity of Bacon's day. The feast is called "a most natural, pious, and reverend custom" (472). It is a celebration in honor of any man, called a Tirsan, who has thirty living descendants who are more than three years old. It begins with "divine service" and ends with the singing of hymns. Some of these praise Adam and Noah for their accomplishments in peopling the world. Some praise Abraham, "the Father of the Faithful," who peopled the household of God. The rest are hymns of thanksgiving specifically for the birth of Christ, "in whose birth the births of all are only blessed." The Tirsan then retires to his "private prayers." He then bestows his blessings (473, 475).

The rich description of the event distracts, however, from the true character of the institution. Emphasis is on physical reproduction, not spiritual regeneration. Hence, Adam and Noah are prominent. It is not Adam's moral lapse that is stressed, but his generative accomplishment. Attention is on Noah's fatherhood, not his faith and righteousness. It is not the cross of Christ and his empty tomb that they celebrate, but only his nativity.[26] As it were, there is Christmas, but no Easter. The Tirsan's blessing asks for a long and happy life; in other words, what Bensalemite science offers. It is no surprise, therefore, that the reference to piety at the beginning of the feast's account drops out and is replaced by "obedience," specifically "to the order of nature." Finally, even "reverence" disappears, and the feast is said to be only "a solemnity wherein nature did so much preside" (472–73, 476). The people of Bensalem are not divided by doctrine, because there is no doctrine. Partly because of this, there is civil peace. But is there peace with God?

Finally, we encounter the Father of Salomon's House, the most reverend of all the Bensalemites. Unlike the governor of

26. Innes, "Bacon's *New Atlantis*," 21.

the Stranger's House, however, he is not identified as holding a religious office. His appearance and behavior are the most religious of anyone's, and yet his office is that of scientist. But this "Father" is no mere administrator or civil servant. He travels with all the pomp that would attend a prince and the solemnity suited to a prelate. He combines both high religious and high political authority. Two footmen precede him in the procession, carrying two symbols of ecclesiastical authority: "the one a crosier, the other a pastoral staff like a sheep-hook" (479). He gives three blessings: one in procession to the crowds, one in private audience to the European strangers, and a final one to the narrator alone as he commissions him to take the good news of modern science to the world. The strangers, following instructions, bow low before him, though whether in reverence for his religious authority or in submission to his political authority is not clear. In private audience, he asks God's blessing on the narrator and, in priestly fashion, calls him "son."

He then bestows the "greatest jewel" he possesses: not the gospel, but "the true state of Salomon's House" (480). But in the name of what "God" does this Father speak, and what blessedness does this "God" offer? Although the Father discloses the true state of Salomon's House "for the love of God and men," the House itself takes as its end merely "the enlarging of the bounds of Human Empire." This is not done for the glory of God, nor for the spreading of the gospel and the dominion of righteousness, but only "to the effecting of all things possible," without any word regarding moral guidance, whether divine or otherwise.

Christian appearance conceals a civil religion that is by design subordinate to the needs of a uniquely scientific society. The Jews who remain in Bensalem, for example, "may the better" follow their religion only because they are civil about it. Their nonconformity is tolerable because of their conformity to Bensalemite principles, because they love Bensalem and its provisions more than they do their religion. Bensalem's surface religious liberality masks a more fundamental illiberality. Of course, the situation of the Jews in Bensalem is Bacon's general formula for religious peace in the modern, technocratic, personal-security state.

The religion that bears the name of him who said, "Do not think that I have come to bring peace to the earth. I have not come to bring peace, but a sword" (Matt. 10:34), is made civil, humane, and inoffensive. The offence of the cross is removed by expunging the concepts of sin and redemption. Thus, the reduction of Christianity to a universalistic moralism with a veneer of its original character serves the political goal of civil peace. It is only when men shall love first the kingdom of Bensalem and its happiness that peace on earth shall be added unto them.

Civil Peace

The people of Bensalem are exceptionally well behaved. They have no church, but also no need of shepherding. It is a "land of angels," a picture of heaven (463). Even bribery is unthinkable. "What? Twice paid!" (461). But this is not from virtue. They are merely "civil." As the Europeans proceed to the Strangers' House, they are greeted by townspeople "on both sides standing in a row; but in so civil a fashion, as if it had been not to wonder at us but to welcome us" (460). They perform like obedient children lining up to greet company. As a Father of Salomon's House parades through the streets for the first time in thirty-seven years, the narrator is struck with the orderliness of the crowds:

> The street was wonderfully well-kept: so that there was never any army had their men stand in better battle-array, than the people stood. The windows likewise were not crowded, but every one stood in them as if they had been placed (479).

The apartments they provided for the exhausted Europeans were furnished "civilly." The Adam and Eve Pools, an arrangement to facilitate marital stability by permitting one's friend to view a prospective mate bathing and alert him or her about a potentially displeasing blemish, is "a more civil way." These "civil" ways are efficient in providing for basic needs and in governing the passions by satisfying them.[27] They suit people and arrange circumstances for the needs of peaceful, efficiently functioning society.

Following Machiavelli's counsel, which Bacon held in high esteem, the people on the island both love and fear their Bensalem, and so are easily governed. By its great power over nature, the Bensalemite state provides bountifully for the people who, in turn, love the state for its provision and fear it for its power. Unlike Machiavelli , however, Bacon gives greater place to love. But the fear is real and effective. People are regimented. There is occasional, shadowy reference to "the state" and "a king," but we see neither. Salomon's House appears to be the ultimate civil authority. It is the Father of Salomon's House who announces the repeal of the ancient and fundamental law concerning secrecy and strangers, apparently on his own authority or on the authority he shares with others in the Order (488).[28] Speaking in his own name, he says, "I give thee leave to publish it," namely this account of the learning and activities of Salomon's House that he has disclosed to the narrator. He does not say "in the King's name" or "by the power invested in me by the state of Bensalem." Bacon fully intended that politics should come within the scope of his new, conquering science and that political affairs be directed by the science of politics. This council of episcipo-scientists governs as a technocracy using the moral

27. Robert K. Faulkner, *Francis Bacon and the Project of Progress* (Lanham, MD: Rowman & Littlefield, 1993), 247.
28. Paterson, "On the Role of Christianity in the Political Philosophy of Francis Bacon," 438.

and civil science with which they have conquered human nature, rendering people "civil."

The people love their nation and are at peace with one another ostensibly because the Bensalemite arrangement keeps them satisfied and "happy." Solamona, Bensalem's ancient founder, "was wholly bent to make his kingdom and people happy." The means to achieve this was "happily established" in his day, which predated by centuries the arrival of Christianity (469–70). The European narrator calls Bensalem "this happy and holy ground." At every Feast of the Family, an especially high occasion, the herald declares merely, "Happy are the people of Bensalem" (463, 474). Repeated reference to the people's happiness suggests beatitude, a realized eschatology.[29] Here again is the hope of Bacon's science. The Christian hope is a state of peace and joy in which "death shall be no more, neither shall there be mourning, nor crying, nor pain anymore, for the former things have passed away" (Rev. 21:4). But relieved of these torments, the redeemed sing, "Blessed is he whose help is the God of Jacob, whose hope is in the LORD his God" (Ps. 146:5). Bacon appeals to us, however, to discern and embrace this new hope, a more easily obtainable and immediately satisfying promise. The conditions for its realization are found in a reformation of learning and of people's general orientation toward nature. The conditions for Bensalem's happiness are thus universally reproducible and reasonably attainable.

Conclusion

Broadly speaking, *New Atlantis* presents two competing hopes based on competing kingdoms: the Christian kingdom of

29. Eric Voegelin wrote extensively against the modern hope as an "immanentization of the Christian eschaton" in *The New Science of Politics* (Chicago: University of Chicago Press, 1952), 121.

God and the Baconian kingdom of man or of nature. On their sixth day, at the book's middle point,[30] after seeing the humanity and civility of Bensalem and all its marvels, and after hearing how it was founded and how Christianity came to its shores, the Europeans declare their liberation. They are converted:

> We took ourselves now for free men, seeing there was no danger of our utter perdition; and lived most joyfully, going abroad and seeing what was to be seen in the city and places adjacent within our tedder; and obtaining acquaintance with many of the city, not of the meanest quality; at whose hands we found such humanity, and such a freedom and desire to take in strangers as it were into their bosom, as was enough to make us forget all that was dear to us in our own countries. . . . If there be a mirror in the world worthy to hold men's eyes, it is that country. (472)

At first appearance, "free" is taken to mean "free to roam" ("going abroad"), but they are still tethered, to use Bacon's word. Are they merely free from fear of execution (461–62)? The reference to "perdition" suggests it is more than that, but the word seems out of place. Up to a certain point in the story, it is from Bensalem that they wish to be freed, so they can return to Europe: "And whether ever we shall see Europe, God only knoweth" (461). Metaphorically, these Europeans travelers—sojourners or wanderers (Ps. 119:19; 1 Peter 2:11)—represent Christians. Europe, in the particular context of this drama, represents the heavenly Christian hope, the home they long to see.

In due course, however, the travelers opt for Bensalem. Their hearts too have journeyed, and they clamor to stay. They have forgotten all they formerly loved in Europe. Even the Christianity

---

30. Weinberger, "Science and Rule," 872–73.

they practiced there no longer governs their hearts or informs their views. They now, consequently, fear no divine judgment—"perdition"—and seek no divine reward. Salvation comes by neither faith nor good behavior,[31] but only from the riches of a Salomon's House, if a people should be so blessed as to have a "divine instrument" (469) like Solamona to bring it into being. This experience of Bensalem has changed them forever. They can never go back, having tasted so much of what Baconianism makes possible. When they opt to remain in Bensalem, they opt to be travelers no more, to renounce Christianity and its hope, thinking themselves to have found its immediate realization.

Bacon intends that we, like the travelers, be converted or reoriented. In these modern times, we have turned from virtue—moral, intellectual, spiritual—as a widely recognized goal (in principle, if not always in practice) to baser, though legitimate, concerns for bodily well-being. As the travelers have been changed and are no longer the men they were, so we have been shaped by our commitment to, dependence on, and hope in Bacon's sovereign science. The benefits we enjoy from this are far from trivial: infant survival and comfortable longevity, as well as cars, computers, and broadly enjoyed bounty. Bacon must not be denied his due. His accomplishment has been heroic, and its effect humane. It is, however, precisely because it is so impressive and so attractive that the cost is so difficult to see and the alternative to remember.

Although the European travelers are mesmerized by how superhumanly perfect the land is, Bacon himself is more sober. Dark features lurk beneath the surface of the tale: unaccountable deception and potentially tyrannical control (484, 486). The hope embodied in Bensalem is a "vision" calculated to inspire

---

31. "Let us so behave ourselves as we may be at peace with God, and may find grace in the eyes of this people" (*NA* 461–62).

bold intellectuals and youthful adventurers and to enlist the ambitious, the humane, and even the godly behind this great enterprise. But the brightness of the vision obscures what Bacon has concealed for the sober reader.[32]

As for Bacon's bright promises, they remain ultimately unfulfilled. In response to the Christian gospel, he promises contentment: "Happy are the people of Bensalem." The Christian hope is the *summum bonum*, the final and deepest satisfaction of the human heart, to enjoy God forever, to rest in him. Bacon explicitly promises an earthly realization of this eternal Sabbath (*GI* 85), but is there finality? Is there peace? If the Bensalemites were a "satisfied" people, there would be massive layoffs at Salomon's House. Perhaps Bacon does not believe such "satisfaction" is possible. Perhaps, like his philosophical son, Thomas Hobbes,[33] he believed there is no *summum bonum*, but only a *summum malum*, death, especially premature, violent death. If so, the greatest human hope would be a comfortable and secure existence extended indefinitely with the hope of resurrection in the event of an accident, both by artificial means.

32. Robert K. Faulkner, "Visions and Powers," 112, 124. Faulkner argues that the hope is to some extent intentionally untrue. "Are not these solid powers of mastery in fact deceptions of the mind, that is, promises of satisfaction that cannot fully satisfy, but which, like the pillar of light, can serve as baits whereby the purveyors of science can win people to a new faith" (*Francis Bacon and the Project of Progress*, 253). Essay No. 58, "Of Vicissitude of Things," suggests that science in its old age can exhaust learning, a thought that can make one "giddy." Regarding immortality and resurrection, Bacon suggests its possibility in several texts, such as "Orpheus" in *Of the Wisdom of the Ancients*, yet it remains to be seen in Bensalem, even though Baconian science has been established there for 1,900 years.

33. John Aubrey reports, "Mr Thomas Hobbes (Malmesburiensis) was beloved by his Lordship, who was wont to have him walk with him, in his delicate groves, where he did meditate: and when a notion darted into his mind, Mr Hobbes was presently to write it downe: and his Lordship was wont to say that he did it better than anyone els about him: for that, many times when he read their notes, he scarce understood what they writt, because they understood it not clearly themselves" (*Brief Lives*, ed. John Buchanan-Brown [London: Penguin, 2000], 25–26).

Perhaps the hope Bacon intended exists on different levels. For the many, there will be ever-increasing comforts and security. For the ambitious few, the knowers, the men of science, there will be honor and rule. The highest hope above all may be the hope of only one man: the man whose followers are as many as those who practice and benefit from the advancement of learning and whose glory is as great and everlasting as the progress of that advancement. Perhaps the only immortality Bacon truly expected is that of everlasting glory, the name above all names that belongs only to the father of blessings, the benefactor of the human race, the inventor of the very means of inventions. But even this hope, Bacon's personal hope, has fallen short of expectations.

4

THE PROBLEM OF
BACON'S PROJECT

The enormous success of Bacon's project has brought over-
whelming benefits—medical marvels, an agricultural revolution,
global telecommunications, steam power, electric power, nuclear
power, computing power. These benefits have, however, come
at a cost. Robert Faulkner, in his penetrating work on Bacon's
artful and revolutionary project, remarks soberly: "It seems that
a thoughtful citizen of a modern country must be prepared to
defend the benefits of progress, or at least to reconsider them
while being aware of the defects as well as the advantages."[1] This
side of Adam's fall, every benefit comes with a cost.

People are ambivalent toward the regime of modern science.
Precisely because of the extraordinary pace of technological
advance, we are generally discontent with our mastery of things,
impatient with the speed and capability of our computerized

1. Robert K. Faulkner, *Francis Bacon and the Project of Progress* (Lanham, MD:
Rowman & Littlefield, 1993), 3.

devices and with the current state of medical science. The more we control the world, the more we feel we need to control it, the more anxiety we feel over our inability to control it, over the uncontrolled unpleasantness or even just the inconvenience of life. First World problems succeed Third World problems, and we cannot bear them. Modern, affluent societies have high rates of suicide, depression, and drug use, yet we harbor great optimism for future advances. The modern irony is that the more we advance in our conquest, the greater our optimism and the greater, in turn, our discontent.

Our view of science and its promises is complicated. We "believe" in science, which is to say we hang our hopes for future conquest of current evils on those who are busy in scientific research and technological development. And yet we also fear. We see this in the tradition of popular literature and films that tap into our fear of techno-dystopias (Huxley's *Brave New World*, 1932; *Gattaca*, 1997; *The Matrix*, 1999, 2003), mad scientists (Shelley's *Frankenstein*, 1818, and the Boris Karloff film adaptation, 1931; Stevenson's *Dr Jekyll and Mr Hyde*, 1886; *Captain America*, 2011), and science that slips beyond the control of the scientists themselves (*The Fly*, 1958; *The Terminator*, 1984; *Jurassic Park*, 1993).

Bacon calls these scientists to benevolence. In *New Atlantis*, he pictures them as kindly and humane. For us, the scientist (whatever the field) embodies the enterprise of science as a whole. In scientific civilization, it is they—taken together, generation after generation—who love us and take care of us. They are prophets of nature, priestly intermediaries between "the mind and things," kingly subduers of nature's merciless indifference, leading her captive in our service. Collectively, they replace Christ as savior. We expect their benevolence, yet we fear their betrayal. Many an action hero in pop culture is fighting a criminally mad scientist or a government employing technologies of control for at best a misguided understanding of the common good and at worst the selfish advantage of those in control.

In fact, benevolence is no more likely in scientists than in nonscientists and has no intrinsic connection with the scientific enterprise. Scientists themselves, publicly accepted as reason incarnate, have shown themselves to be subject to passions like everyone else, even in their research. Global warming research has been repeatedly exposed as politically driven, especially when politically interested funding has been involved.[2] Typically, young people go into the hard sciences for the joy of figuring things out, of discovery, of conquest. The driving desire is what the Greeks called *thumos*, the warrior spirit and the desire for distinction, not *agape*. Even in *New Atlantis*, Bensalem motivates its great discoverers with high honors.

This popular skepticism comes in part from a record of science's evil applications. Eugenics was considered the cutting edge of enlightened, scientific progress for the half century prior to World War II. The scientific establishment of the day aggressively advocated eugenic progress. The Eugenics Record Office was established to facilitate better "breeding" among us. Charles Davenport, its director and formerly professor of zoology at the University of Chicago, preached, "Man is an organism, an animal, and the laws of improvement of corn and of race horses hold true for him also." Edward Conklin, a Princeton biologist, lamented that, though nature killed off the worst "defectives," many survive in modern society, "preserved by charity, and . . . are allowed to reproduce." It was common to refer to the less "fit" as defectives, weeds, apes, refuse, and parasites. These were respectable scientific assessments. Critics were called "antiscience reactionaries" and "religious zealots" standing in the way

2. D. C. Innes, "On the Environment," in Lisa Sharon Harper and D. C. Innes, *Left, Right, and Christ* (Boise, ID: Russell Media, 2011), 213–16.

of "progress."[3] Nazi experimentation on Jewish prisoners and the Tuskegee syphilis experiments on African Americans were also just science doing its business. The gene-editing technology CRISPR-Cas9 holds tremendous potential for remedying serious ills, but holds equally great potential for horrific abuse.

Modern science as Bacon presents it and as we have inherited and embraced it at least in spirit, has two problems that correspond to the two hopes it holds for us: the hope-as-method and the hope-as-goal. The problem with restricting logic-for-truth to hope-as-method is that it leaves us without any knowable moral guidance. Philosopher of modernity Hans Jonas observes, "The scientist himself is by his science no more qualified than others to discern, nor is he more disposed to care for, the good of mankind. Benevolence must be called in from the outside to supplement the knowledge acquired through theory: it does not flow from theory itself."[4] But this restriction of knowing to modern methods of science shutters Salomon's House against any outside influence, including that of the gospel. Without this governing influence, we end up, alongside our comfortable longevity, in eugenic engineering and behavioral conditioning, Aldous Huxley's World State and B.F. Skinner's *Walden Two*. The problem with the hope-as-goal—technologically empowered human mastery for perpetual and universal human comfort—is that it instrumentalizes the world even as it inflates our sense of divine power. It operates at least as powerfully on us as we operate on the world through it, and it concentrates power even as it amplifies it with dangerous, tyrannical results. These two problems, scientism and technology, are the

3. John G. West, *Darwin Day in America: How Our Politics and Culture Have Been Dehumanized in the Name of Science* (Wilmington, DE: ISI Books, 2007), 130, 129, 139.
4. Hans Jonas, *The Phenomenon of Life: Toward a Philosophical Biology* (New York: Harper & Row, 1966), 195.

sources of our ambivalence toward science, the fear that lingers around the realization of Bacon's hope.

Scientism

Bacon's proposed new way of reasoning about the world goes beyond a more effective science. It is "scientism,"[5] the functionally unnecessary and philosophically unjustified doctrine that genuine knowledge, regardless of the field of inquiry, comes only by the method and instruments of the modern physical sciences. He announced this in the opening affirmation of *The New Organon*: "Man, being the servant and interpreter of Nature, can do and understand so much and so much only as he has observed in fact or in thought of the course of nature. Beyond this he neither knows anything nor can do anything."

Bacon expected that as the new method of science gained authority and as its benefits multiplied, this way of reasoning would come to be accepted as logic-for-truth itself.[6] The received method of reason, Aristotle's logic of the syllogism, he viewed as valid—Bacon used it freely and masterfully, not only in the *Essays* but throughout his works—but only as logic-for-persuasion because it cannot penetrate the deeper recesses of nature to discover her useful secrets. "For the logic which is received, though it be very properly applied to civil business and

5. See Bruce L. Gordon and William A. Dembski, eds., *The Nature of Nature: Examining the Role of Naturalism in Science* (Wilmington, DE: ISI Books, 2011); Michael D. Aeschliman, *The Restitution of Man: C.S. Lewis and the Case Against Scientism* (Grand Rapids: Eerdmans, 1983); John G. West, ed., *The Magician's Twin: C. S. Lewis on Science, Scientism, and Society* (Seattle: Discovery Institute Press, 2012); Neil Postman, *Technopoly: The Surrender of Culture to Technology* (New York: Vintage, 1993).

6. So observed J. Gresham Machen: "No department of knowledge can maintain its isolation from the modern lust of scientific conquest; treaties of inviolability though hallowed by all the sanctions of age-long tradition, are being flung ruthlessly to the winds" (*Christianity and Liberalism* [1923; repr., Grand Rapids: Eerdmans, 1946], 3).

to those arts which rest in discourse and opinion, is not nearly subtle enough to deal with nature" (*GI* 72). It is the master of opinion, not of things.

Implicit in Bacon's distinction between these two forms of reason is what has come to be called the fact-value distinction.[7] Logic-for-truth, the new natural science, discovers "facts." This science includes every discipline of learning that legitimately models itself on the methods of natural science—for example, what we call the "social sciences" like anthropology and economics. Moral, metaphysical, and aesthetic claims, like principles of right, religious beliefs, and judgments of beauty, are, by this standard of knowing, necessarily personal, private judgments. They cannot be anything other than opinions. They are "relative" to the one making the claim, so we call them "values," an inherently relativistic term. They indicate where the one making the judgment places value. They are entirely autobiographical, expressing only what is internal to the one expressing them, but telling us nothing about the way things are in the wider world. This is scientism.

But the wide acceptance of scientism plunges the human race into a moral and spiritual abyss. According to Bruce L. Gordon, "Scientism establishes a hermetic boundary between facts and values that strips all values of their factuality and all facts of any objective noninstrumental valuation. The end result is moral nihilism and the instrumentalization of rationality to subjective ends incapable of objective evaluation in terms of their intrinsic merit."[8] Neither form of reasoning—neither logic-for-truth nor

---

7. The word *fact* comes from the Latin *facere*, meaning "to do" or "to make." Thomas Hobbes, Bacon's celebrated student, taught that we can only understand what we make (*De Homine* X.4–5). Bacon taught that the world can be known only through experiments "made." See also Antonio Perez-Ramos, *Francis Bacon's Idea of Science and the Maker's Knowledge Tradition* (Oxford: Oxford University Press, 1988).

8. Bruce L. Gordon, "The Rise of Naturalism and Its Problematic Role in Science and Culture," in *The Nature of Nature*, ed. Gordon and Dembski, 4.

logic-for-persuasion—is a form of moral reasoning. Neither one can ascertain moral principles by which one can judge whether a course of action is right or wrong.

Yet these unprovable "values" pertain to what is indisputably most important to us. We like our cars, for example, but we are more deeply affected if someone vandalizes or steals our car, doing us injustice, or, more so, hits and kills a loved one with a car. Fundamentally, our hearts long not for power over nature, but, aided by that power, to dwell comfortably and perpetually in love and justice. Science can control, but it cannot satisfy.

Nonetheless, Bacon calls for this method or logic, oriented as it is toward mastery, to be applied to moral and political questions:

> It may also be asked (in the way of doubt rather than objection) whether I speak of natural philosophy only, or whether I mean that the other sciences, logic, ethics, and politics, should be carried on by this method. Now I certainly mean what I have said to be understood of them all; and as the common logic, which governs by the syllogism, extends not only to natural but to all sciences, so does mine also, which proceeds by induction, embrace everything. (*NO* I.127)

This raises the obvious difficulty of moral guidance, not only in these particular fields, but also in the project as a whole. Applying the method of natural science to morals and politics is, to say the least, inappropriate. Human behavior is not like the operations of inanimate matter or even of our animate bodies. Unlike the nonhuman universe, we are moral in character, that is, directed toward ends properly understood in terms of what is just and unjust, good and evil, godly and ungodly. The older tradition did not face this difficulty. Ancient philosophy was oriented toward the good—for example, the good life or the good society—and this good was believed to be knowable. The new logic, by contrast, has nothing within itself to provide moral guidance. It restricts all human knowledge to that of causes, a concept that Bacon effectively transforms.

Prior to Bacon, the word *cause* was rich in meaning. According to Aristotle, who serves as the backdrop for all of Bacon's remarks, there were four different causes: material, formal, efficient, and final (*NO* II.2).[9] Everything has matter and form. Simply speaking, matter provides the potentiality for a thing's existence as well as its individuating principle, whereas form gives it actuality and is the same in all members of the species of which it is the form. Thus, form is not shape, but the definable essence. Matter is not extension, but the substratum of a thing that endures changes of form. These two elements of a body constitute two different kinds of causation, namely, the material and formal causes. Efficient cause is the external agent of change, as the builder is to the house, but it need not be external (nor must all external agents be efficient). It may be identical with another kind of cause, such as the formal, for example, in the case of growth. Lastly, final cause is that toward which a thing is ordered, whether externally, as a knife is to cutting (the knife was made for the purpose of cutting), or internally, as anything is to its perfect embodiment or mature state. Underlying this account is a teleological understanding of nature that sees the world arrayed with purpose, and nature doing "nothing in vain."[10]

Although initially accepting that causes are "not improperly distributed into four kinds," Bacon proceeds either to reject their utility or radically to transform our understanding of them.

9. Aristotle, *Physics* II.7. Cf. Frederick Copleston, *A History of Philosophy*, vol. I, pt. II (New York: Image Books, 1962), 46–56.

10. Aristotle, *On the Soul* (*De Anima*), trans. J. A. Smith, in *The Basic Works of Aristotle*, ed. Richard McKeon (New York: Random House, 1941), 434a31; see also 432b21, and *On the Heavens* (*De Caelo*), 271a33.

Investigation into final causes, he says, "corrupted" philosophy, since they "have relation clearly to the nature of man rather than to the nature of the universe."[11] The study of efficient and material causes he calls "slight and superficial" and relatively useless "to true and active science." He accepts only the formal cause as worthy of study, but only after redefining it.

In Book II of *The New Organon*, appearing to follow Aristotle, Bacon at first identifies form with "true specific difference," calling it also the "nature-engendering nature, or source of emanation" (II.1). Discovering a thing's form in this sense is "the work and aim of human knowledge." But immediately prior to this, he says, "the work and aim of human power" is "to generate or superinduce a new nature or new natures." The reader recalls from the opening of Book I that "Human knowledge and human power meet in one; for where the [formal] cause is not known the effect cannot be produced" (*NO* I.3). Knowledge of form provides understanding of the working of things—what it is by which a body or substance has particular characteristics—and thus empowers us to change one thing into another or, in short, "to command nature in action" (*GI* 77). This understanding of things solely in terms of the forces and mechanics of their operation—as matter in motion—is far from what Aristotle and the medieval tradition recognized as form and cause. At the end of *The New Organon* II.2, Bacon notes that he adopted the word "form" because "it has grown into use and become familiar"— in other words, to take advantage of the authority attached to the word. People will be less on guard against a familiar though completely redefined word than they would against a wholly new word in addition to the idea.

This transformed and more restrictive understanding of causality incapacitates science for recognizing or submitting to

11. *NO* I.48; cf. I.65.

moral purpose. Nonetheless, the enterprise of science and the power it unlocks and unleashes require guidance of some sort.

Nature is disqualified from supplying man's moral boundaries or his *telos* because the only natural law is "the laws of nature," which are strictly operational, not normative. The only reason for "obeying" nature—following its rules—is to command it (*NO* I.3). Happiness, if it is possible, comes only by "the power of man . . . emancipated and freed from the common course of nature" (*NO* II.17). Nature does not provide for man. Instead, man provides for himself by harnessing reluctant and reticent nature. Yet Bacon calls for the development of moral and political sciences after the model of the natural sciences, to discover the cause and effect of moral and political behavior (*NO* I.127). Only with this conquest of specifically human nature will man be able adequately to provide for his comfortable security in this world.

Bacon tells us in *The New Organon* that the powerful new science "will be governed by right reason and true religion" (I.129, *recta ratio et sana religio*).[12] But reason as Bacon represents it to us is incapable of discerning moral ends, proper uses, or any directing principle. It is strictly calculative, means-end thinking. It can determine what is, but it cannot get from there to what ought to be. It can survey what people think about what is right, it can observe the prevailing and most powerful passions, but it cannot provide the rational principle by which those passions may be judged and ordered. It could provide a basis for confident prediction of most people's behavior under specified conditions and thus guidance for prudent personal behavior and effective government policy. In this understanding, economics—the study of choice-making, understood as interest-maximization—would

12. Spedding's translation here is highly interpretive. What he renders "true religion" Bacon calls *sana religio*, "sound (or healthy) religion."

replace moral theology and normative moral philosophy as the rational basis for directing both our personal lives and our common life. In a work that explains and defends the new method of logic-for-truth, Bacon surely understood that science cannot be governed by right reason when our only rational access to truth of any kind is by that selfsame science.

Bacon tells us that "moral philosophy . . . to the heathen was as theology to us" (*NO* I.79). That is, in Christendom, theology is the primary source for moral understanding. But after Bacon's "total reconstruction (*instauratio*) of sciences, arts, and all human knowledge raised upon the proper foundations" (*GI* 66), "moral and political philosophy" will be "nourished by natural philosophy," which he calls, not a handmaiden to anything, but "the great mother of the sciences" and the "root" from which the other fields of inquiry must not be torn if they are to grow (*NO* I.79, 80).

In noting that moral philosophy was to the ancients what theology is to us, Bacon could mean that theology is reducible to moral philosophy and religion to a kind of moralism. Conversely, he could mean that, for the pagans, moral philosophy was a kind of religion or theology, and that virtue was worshipped among them. If he intends his readers to understand theology as merely moral in its concern, he leaves nothing for theology once moral studies have been regrounded on natural philosophy. If Bacon has paralleled moral philosophy and theology, then since the former is to be grounded in natural philosophy, the latter must be grounded in the same.

Just nine aphorisms later, Bacon reaffirms philosophy's role as handmaid to theology, except that standing in for Lady Philosophy is natural philosophy in its new Baconian form. This is an important difference. Philosophy has always helped theology in interpreting Scripture and formulating doctrine. But Bacon's natural philosophy will not merely provide natural discoveries

to aid our understanding of certain passages and practical doc-
trines. It will supply a new logic for theological as well as moral
and political thinking. Once scientific thinking becomes the only
legitimate logic-for-truth, there is no alternative. Bacon made the
same point in *The Advancement of Learning*. Explaining how philosophy serves faith and religion, he piously describes the two
books of God, "the Scriptures, revealing the will of God, and
then the creatures expressing his power; whereof the latter is a
key unto the former: . . . opening our understanding to conceive
the true sense of the Scriptures, by the general notions of reason
and rules of speech" (153). This seems uncontroversial until one
realizes that by "philosophy" he means this power-oriented natural philosophy. But in that case, who is governing whom?

As for sound (healthy) religion, his Christian readership
would have understood religion that is faithful to the teachings of Scripture. But reasoning about what the Bible says for
the direction of our lives depends on that same logic-for-truth.
If Scripture, to be faithfully expounded, requires right reason
understood as the new science, and if Scripture and the *sana
religio* proceeding from it are to govern the discoveries of the
new science, then the new science becomes its own overseer,
a judge in its own trial, the very objection Bacon lays against
any criticism of his science that comes from the old logic (*NO*
I.33).[13] Reading the Bible with this sort of "right reason" is what
we know today as theological liberalism. This tradition of standing over the Bible in the position of natural scientist, not living
under it as humble believer, began immediately after Bacon's

---

13. Thomas Fowler understands Bacon to be contradicting himself; that is, while
seeking to liberate natural philosophy from theology, he subordinates it as a handmaid. His response is typical of those who carelessly underestimate Bacon's philosophical thoroughness: "But then at this stage in the history of ethical thought, we
must not expect consistency" (*Bacon's Novum Organum*, 2nd ed. [Oxford: Clarendon
Press, 1889], 21).

death with Thomas Hobbes (1588–1679), followed by Baruch Spinoza (1632–77), Pierre Bayle (1647–1706), Friedrich Schleiermacher (1768–1834), David Strauss (1808–74), and Rudolf Bultmann (1884–1976).[14] And it continues. This theological stance judges matters by the measure of reason and experience and thus rejects, as Machen put it, "any entrance of the creative power of God (as distinguished from the ordinary course of nature) in connection with the origin of Christianity."[15] One theologian characterized this Baconian science of Scripture as "a technology of criticism in the spirit of the Enlightenment that does not submit itself to God speaking in the Scriptures."[16] Scripture provides no basis for knowledge. Hence, we cannot join with Job in saying, "I know that my Redeemer lives" (Job 19:25), but only with Solomon when he says, "The living know that they will die" (Eccl. 9:5)—and we're working on that. Bacon denies that the new learning in any way touches upon the mysteries of the faith (*GI* 74), but it is only because these mysteries cannot be objects of knowledge. In adding "sound religion" to "right reason" as guide for science, Bacon clearly expected that as this understanding of *recta ratio* became more widely employed in biblical studies and theological reasoning, Christianity would not be replaced, but merely reinterpreted and redirected, taking on the civil or culturally supportive role we see it has in Bensalem.

14. Interestingly, the Old School Presbyterians at Princeton embraced the Baconian spirit that was so popular at the time. Charles Hodge wrote, "The Bible is to the theologian what nature is to the man of science. It is his store-house of facts." James Alexander wrote as one schooled at the feet of Lord Verulam: "The theologian should proceed in his investigation precisely as the chemist or the botanist proceeds." This is "the method which bears the name of Bacon." Quoted in Nancy Pearcey, *Total Truth: Liberating Christianity from Its Cultural Captivity* (Wheaton, IL: Crossway, 2004), 299.

15. Machen, *Christianity and Liberalism*, 2.

16. Clark Pinnock, "This Treasure in Earthen Vessels: The Inspiration and Interpretation of the Bible," *Sojourners*, October 1980.

The conquest of nature is a liberation from the necessities of toil and the indifference of fortune—what Bacon called "the relief of our estate." But because Bacon has truncated and reoriented all logic-for-truth, his promised conquest decouples human power from any source of moral governance. Lesslie Newbigin, speaking of Enlightenment rationalism in general, writes:

> Reason, so understood, is sovereign in this enterprise. It cannot bow before any authority other than what it calls the facts. No alleged divine revelation, no tradition however ancient, and no dogma however hallowed has the right to veto its exercise.[17]

But this moral decoupling is understood as a moral liberation, as victory in a war of human independence. George Grant states it pointedly:

> The liberation of human desiring from any supposed excluding claim, so that it is believed that we freely create values, is a face of the same liberation in which men overcame chance by technology—the liberty to make happen what we want to make happen.[18]

Although some see a moral and spiritual crisis in this, with the capacity to destabilize the very possibility of personal well-being and a shared life, it is precisely what others like about scientific civilization. They see a humanizing emancipation from moral constraint, from the arbitrary values of their neighbors and ancestors, whether based in religion, nature, or tradition.

---

17. Lesslie Newbigin, *Foolishness to the Greeks* (Grand Rapids: Eerdmans, 1986), 25.

18. George Parkin Grant, "'The Computer Does Not Impose on Us the Ways It Should Be Used,'" in *The George Grant Reader*, ed. William Christian and Sheila Grant (Toronto: University of Toronto Press, 1998), 430.

As Bacon's naturalistic principles gain universal authority, the humanitarian goal of his project disappears, or at least its grounding. Philosophical naturalism[19]—the conceptual presupposition of which is that everything operates on, and is fully explicable in terms of, physical laws and forces (a form of materialism), and the epistemological form of which is scientism—is now regarded as essential to scientific investigation. Anyone who is willing to give safe harbor to teleology, to recognizing purpose and obvious handiwork by a supernatural, intelligent Being, is importing "pseudoscience" into an otherwise respectable pursuit and, quite frankly, endangering the human race—or so the story goes. This restrictive view of science excludes human exceptionalism, the view that human beings have a special value, whether because of the *imago dei* and their special creation on the sixth day or the recognition that they are rational animals with capacity for moral judgments and philosophic understanding. Without a grounded notion of human exceptionalism, Bacon's domination of nature can have no humanitarian, much less charitable, directedness except insofar as it happens to coincide with the personal interests of the scientists or their employers.

Consider Charles Darwin, who gave us the consummate science of man. He was a committed Baconian. He made a point of saying that he "worked upon the true principles of Baconian induction."[20] Accordingly, his evolutionary theory was consciously naturalistic and anti-teleological (unlike the theories of his contemporary evolutionist, Alfred Russell Wallace). He viewed the inherent worth of human beings as no different

19. One of C. S. Lewis's great projects was to expose and refute philosophical naturalism. See *The Abolition of Man* (1943); *That Hideous Strength* (1945); *Miracles* (1947), chaps. 1–6; "De Futilitate" and "Funeral for a Great Myth," in *Christian Reflections* (1967).

20. Charles Darwin, *The Autobiography of Charles Darwin*, ed. Nora Barlow (New York: Norton, 1969), 119.

from that of any beast, fish, or insect. This followed logically. His current defenders like to distance Darwinism from Social Darwinism, as though it were a political perversion of honest science. But Darwin himself voiced it in *The Descent of Man*:

> We civilised men . . . do our utmost to check the process of elimination; we build asylums for the imbecile, the maimed, and the sick; we institute poor-laws; and our medical men exert their utmost skill to save the life of every one to the last moment. There is reason to believe that vaccination has preserved thousands, who from a weak constitution would formerly have succumbed to small-pox. Thus, the weak members of civilised societies propagate their kind. No one who has attended to the breeding of domestic animals will doubt that this must be highly injurious to the race of man.[21]

With the rejection of human exceptionalism, even the *imago dei*, some people (the few and powerful) will inevitably come to reject the human exceptionalism of other people (the many powerless) and use them freely for their selfish advantage. Without religious grounds for valuing people or without some morally shaping influence by a good culture, killing off the insane and disabled will seem perfectly reasonable.

This is precisely what happened in the early twentieth century, sanctioned by the United States Supreme Court in *Buck v. Bell*, a case in which Justice Oliver Wendell Holmes wrote for a nearly unanimous court in 1927, "It is better for all the world if, instead of waiting to execute degenerate offspring from crime or to let them starve for their imbecility, society can prevent those who are manifestly unfit from continuing their kind."[22]

21. Charles Darwin, *The Descent of Man* (repr., New York: Penguin, 2004), 159. See also John G. West, "The Church of Darwin," *First Things*, June 2015.
22. *Buck v. Bell*, 274 U.S. 200 (1927), 207.

This was received across the country as the voice, not only of law, but of science. "By 1940, almost thirty-six thousand men and women had been sterilized in public institutions across the United States. . . . All told, government-sponsored sterilizations took place in thirty states, and 46 percent of the operations were performed on those classified as 'feeble-minded.'"[23] Now, in the twenty-first century, people of naturalistic thinking are not denying rights, but expanding them to other life forms and even to inanimate formations: animals, plants, and rivers.[24] But when plants are seen as having inherent "rights" on a level with humans, the currency of the term becomes debased to the point of uselessness. Rights evaporate. We may treat plants more like humans, but more likely and more often we will treat humans more like plants, or at least some humans.

B. F. Skinner, a man thoroughly embedded in the scientistic view, saw that science—political and moral science in particular—is ultimately incompatible with human freedom and dignity. If we could understand scientifically what we call happiness (a feeling of euphoria?), we could supply it reliably through technology, maybe in a pill (call it soma) or in the intelligent structuring of our environment and daily activity through technocratic government:

> What we need is a technology of behavior. We could solve
> our problems quickly enough if we could adjust the growth
> of the world's population as precisely as we adjust the course

---

23. West, *Darwin Day in America*, 141. For the progression from American Darwinism to Nazi atrocities, see Richard Weikart, *From Darwin to Hitler: Evolutionary Ethics, Eugenics, and Racism in Germany* (New York: Palgrave Macmillan, 2004).

24. Wesley J. Smith, *A Rat Is a Pig Is a Dog Is a Boy* (New York: Encounter Books, 2010), and *The War on Humans* (Seattle: Discovery Institute Press, 2014). In 2017, New Zealand's parliament granted the Whanganui River the legal rights of a person. https://e360.yale.edu/digest/new-zealand-river-legally-granted-same-rights-as-humans. Accessed July 13, 2018.

of a spaceship, or improve agriculture and industry with some of the confidence with which we accelerate high-energy particles, or move toward a peaceful world with something like the steady progress with which physics has approached absolute zero (even though both remain presumably out of reach). But a behavioral technology comparable in power and precision to physical and biological technology is lacking.[25]

Given the way our public discourse is governed by the metaphysical presuppositions of scientism, there is no reason science should not replace politics. Why should the rule of social engineers not replace the self-government of citizens?

Richard Kennington says, "The *New Atlantis* suffices to show that for Bacon longevity and vigor of bodily existence, as well as comfortable and affluent life, are greater goods than political freedom."[26] The consummated kingdom of nature will be technocratic, not democratic. Once happiness becomes a technical problem with a technical solution, freedom is unnecessary and counterproductive, the pathological obsession of people who don't know what's good for them. In Bacon's Bensalem, the government is humane and parentlike, and everyone is "happy," as we are told repeatedly.[27] Any unprovided need is the daily research concern of the kingdom's central institution. But the scientific administration that supplies these wonderful modern benefits requires centralized scientific control of all human affairs for their most perfect provision. Within Bacon's epistemology, which is our modern frame of reference, moral reasoning is not

25. B. F. Skinner, *Beyond Freedom and Dignity* (New York: Bantam Books, 1972), 3–4.
26. Richard Kennington, "Bacon's Humanitarian Revision of Machiavelli," in *On Modern Origins: Essays in Early Modern Philosophy*, by Richard Kennington, ed. Pamela Kraus and Frank Hunt (Lanham, MD: Lexington Books, 2004), 74.
27. *NA* 474; see also 463, 466, 469–70.

for grasping otherwise elusive moral truths, but only for the moral control of people, the control of those who are mastered by those who have themselves mastered this science. Bacon's project culminates in, to paraphrase Tocqueville, soft totalitarianism. For us, it is the administrative state that provides security, devours liberty, and is uncomprehending of accountability. But Bacon thought it was worth it, either for our benefit, his benefit, or both.

Technological science justifies its privileged place among us—its generous funding, its domination of the universities, its intrusive poking into everything—by its benevolent purposes, its commitment to "the relief of our estate." But this is a moral end and, from a scientific point of view, an arbitrary choice. From a strictly scientific point of view, as we currently understand science, the development of technology, whether for broadly relieving misery or for supporting the domination of the few as masters over the many as slaves, is a matter of indifference. Einstein saw this:

> I know that it is a hopeless undertaking to debate about funda-
> mental value judgements. For instance, if someone approves,
> as a goal, the extirpation of the human race from the earth,
> one cannot refute such a viewpoint on rational grounds. But if
> there is agreement on certain goals and values, one can argue
> rationally about the means by which these objectives may be
> attained.[28]

The personal morality of the scientists themselves may bear upon the question, but it would do so, not insofar as they are scien-tists, but insofar as they have been formed in a moral community, whether civic or religious. The moral obligation to apply science

---

28. Albert Einstein, "Freedom and Science," quoted in Charles T. Rubin, *Eclipse of Man* (New York: Encounter Books, 2014), epigraph.

to human benefit, specifically understood as universal comfort and security, is, as such, "unscientific."

If scientism has subverted Christian thinking and Christian civilization, Bacon was a great and subversive thinker. In announcing "a total reconstruction" of "all human knowledge, raised upon the proper foundations" (*GI* 66), he included moral and theological knowledge. The movement from Bacon's works to Skinner and Bultmann, Darwin and Dawkins, was only a matter of time as each generation of Baconians worked out the implications of this project.

Technology

In redirecting all legitimate reason toward the production of useful inventions, Bacon redefined it as technological. The problem of Bacon's project lies not only in the means he advocated for getting to that technology—the scientism—but also in the technology itself.[29] But if technology were simply evil, it would not present us with a problem, but only an imperative: Get rid of it! It is a problem, however, because it is a mixed blessing with which we bless ourselves while bringing new difficulties upon ourselves. Its humane benefits and pleasant advantages are obvious, but the practical arts are inherently double-sided. The power to heal is also the power to kill. The power to broadcast can speak truth as well as falsehood.

Bacon concedes that science can be used for evil, but he responds that because any earthly good can be abused, the

29. For the best treatments of the problem of technology, see Martin Heidegger, *The Question concerning Technology and Other Essays*, trans. William Lovitt (New York: Harper & Row, 1977); Leon Kass, *Life, Liberty and the Defense of Dignity: The Challenge for Bioethics* (San Francisco: Encounter Books, 2002); Postman, *Technopoly*; Jacques Ellul, *The Technological Society*, trans. John Wilkinson (New York: Vintage, 1964); Arthur M. Melzer, Jerry Weinberger, and M. Richard Zinman, eds., *Technology in the Western Political Tradition* (Ithaca, NY: Cornell University Press, 1993).

problem is not unique to the great power over nature his advancement of learning will unlock:

> If the debasement of arts and sciences to purposes of wickedness, luxury, and the like, be made a ground of objection, let no one be moved thereby. For the same may be said of all earthly goods: of wit, courage, strength, beauty, wealth, light itself, and the rest. (*NO* I.129)

But comparing it to just any earthly good distracts not only from the unique way it empowers, but also from the way it changes us—how we see ourselves, our world, and each other.

We speak of technology in two senses. The word as commonly employed designates useful inventions: the wheel, gunpowder, the telephone. But to speak of premodern inventions and mechanical innovations as "technologies" blurs an important distinction. Among "inventions," we may distinguish "tools" (which are not exclusively premodern: the hook-and-eye mousetrap and the folding chair, for example) from (specifically modern) "technologies." We coined the modern word *technology* because of the inadequacy of the old word *invention* to capture what is unique about modern making.

Aristotle observed that "art" (*techne*) is making (as opposed to mere doing) "that is accompanied by true reason" (*logos*)—the activity, for example, of the shoemaker, the cook, or the poet.[30] He would not call what they make "technologies" because every product of a *techne* employs *logos*, as opposed to things that arise naturally because they have their origin in themselves. He would view the term as a redundancy. The difference between what rational creatures have always done in forging tools and

---

30. Aristotle, *Nicomachean Ethics*, trans. Robert C. Bartlett and Susan D. Collins (Chicago: University of Chicago Press, 2011), 1140a10, bk. 6, chap. 4.

using tools to make useful things and what modern science enables us to produce is the difference between ancient art and modern technology. The word *technology* refers primarily to the modern marriage of *techne* (the art or skill of producing something) and *logos* (reason), combining "making" with a particular kind of "knowing," one that comes by reasoning that is only with a view to making. This is what Bacon described in the first four aphorisms of *The New Organon*. George Parkin Grant, an especially insightful philosopher of technology, argues that "this novel relationship stands at the heart of the modern era."[31]

Thus, the secondary sense of the word *technology* indicates the fruit of that marriage, the useful products of that application of reason so understood. These products are typically machines, but may be, for example, computer software, organizational systems, or rhetorical techniques. Bacon recognized the great discoveries and inventions of the past, even in the preceding hundred years: the printing press, the magnetic compass, and gunpowder. But whereas premodern inventions had come about by chance, trial-and-error tinkering, or the practical wisdom of artisans,[32] Bacon anticipated an exponential growth of artful production by understanding the basic operating principles of nature, the forms of things, allowing us to command nature by obeying these forms that nature guards as secrets from clumsy and hasty inquirers. This is what distinguishes the modern marvels to which we give the modern name "technology." It is the Baconian project itself.

One may ask, then, what complaint anyone could have with that.

Technology is not just a tool. It changes how we see everything—ourselves, others, natural things and the things we make,

---

31. Grant, "'The Computer Does Not Impose on Us the Ways It Should Be Used,'" 422.
32. *NO* I.8; *AL* 201.

time, space, and God. This way of thinking about the world leaves us bereft of ability to think of ourselves as human and of our universe as a moral arena and a sanctuary in which to worship its Creator in all we do. It instrumentalizes everything—even ourselves. Technology, writes Leon Kass, is "a way of standing in and toward the world" or, more fully, "the disposition rationally to order and predict and control everything feasible, in order to master fortune and spontaneity, violence and wildness, and to leave nothing to chance, all in the service of human benefit."[33] This is what the Father of Salomon's House meant by "the enlarging of the bounds of Human Empire, to the effecting of all things possible" (*NA* 480). These words express the unique spirit of modern instrumentality that Bacon has bequeathed to us. It pictures the world with neutral instruments on one side and human autonomy on the other, with autonomous will working on the world as object to subjugate it. That view of man as autonomous is characteristically modern.

With a debt to Neil Postman's analysis in *Technopoly*,[34] we may distinguish for the purposes of this study between theological society (medieval Christendom) and technological society (the modern West). In a theological society, the accepted metaphysical and moral beliefs and the authorities responsible for curating them set boundaries for invention and the use of what is invented. We see this today among the Amish, among whom only what is compatible with community and faith is permitted. Consider the recent controversies among us over stem cell research and abortion, and at one time birth control. The controversies indicate the extent to which theological society persists among us. But our cultural, commercial, and academic elites are technological.

33. Kass, *Life, Liberty and the Defense of Dignity*, 33.
34. Postman, *Technopoly*, chap. 2, "From Tools to Technocracy."

A technological society is completely open to possibility. The typical American whom Alexis de Tocqueville described in 1835 captures this spirit: "Nowhere does he see any limit placed by nature to human endeavor; in his eyes something that does not exist is just something that has not been tried."[35] Bacon encouraged this frame of mind in support of his project for the kingdom of man over the universe. The alternative is to understand oneself and the instruments at one's disposal as saturated with, and thus morally bound by, purpose. Things present themselves to us with their various discernable purposes and we misuse them to our harm. That purpose is either in the nature of the natural object or in the human design of an artificial object.

But this view of ourselves as sovereign over our technology and over the universe through our technology is a self-deception. Sober observation reveals that the power of man over nature through technology is, on the one hand, a power our technologies exercise over us by their very nature and, on the other hand, as Lewis says, "a power exercised by some men over other men with Nature as its instrument."[36] Our conquest of nature is reciprocal.

The first underlying domination is a form of technological imperative. This phrase usually indicates that if a technology can be developed and disseminated, it will be. But if it can be, we are told, it also must be. The liberation from all moral reasoning and religious teaching that comes with scientific civilization—the realization of Bensalem—entails that industrial science cannot be questioned in its research and development activities. Indeed, on curiously groundless moral grounds, and regardless of its consequences for society, it must not be questioned.

35. Alexis de Tocqueville, *Democracy in America*, ed. J. P. Mayer, trans. George Lawrence (Garden City, NY: Anchor, 1969), 404.
36. C. S. Lewis, *The Abolition of Man* (1943; repr., New York: Macmillan, 1947), 55.

There is, however, an imperative associated, not with technology's emergence among us, but with its operation upon us. Technology itself changes us in ways that we do not choose and without regard for the requirements of personal well-being or healthy community life. The use of a technology entails certain forms of behavior and thinking, and it suppresses or disinclines us toward others. The printing press expanded human learning and literature in obvious ways, but it also killed oral culture and the common pastime of storytelling that from time immemorial bound one generation to another. It was an unintended consequence, but it was what technology imposed on us by way of use and disinclination to use. The phonograph, the radio, and their technological descendants brought high-fidelity recordings of the most gifted musicians into ordinary living rooms, but, in doing so, killed genuine folk music and the communal life of composing, singing, playing, and dancing. These were, by technological imperative, doomed to exotic oddity.

The enormous human power over the universe that Bacon promises is not, contrary to what he argued, comparable to powers we have always possessed and used either justly or unjustly— strength of body, fairness of face, wealth and station. Power is always someone's power and it is, by the diversity in human faculties, distributed unevenly among us. Technology vastly amplifies that power difference. For example, the difference between a traditional despotism, as evil as that is, and modern totalitarianism is that technology allows a tyrant not only to hold total power but also to exercise total control.[37] This extends not only to controlling people as they are, but also to changing what they are and what future generations will be, if they are allowed to come into being at all.[38] The control of nature necessarily extends

37. Karl A. Wittfogel, *Oriental Despotism: A Comparative Study of Total Power* (New Haven: Yale University Press, 1957), chaps. 4–5.
38. Lewis, *The Abolition of Man*, 59.

itself to the control of specifically human nature for a tyranny more profound than Cyrus the Great ever dreamed possible.

Bringing human beings under the controlling power of science has implications for how we treat people. As this nature-conquering natural science turns to human beings themselves, people come to be viewed not as ends, having value in themselves, but only as means, as useful artifacts, the products of someone's science.[39] What we call the social sciences and the biological sciences, insofar as they bring human behavior under their dominion, eventually dehumanize all of us, both practitioners and those practiced upon. Leon Kass warns us that human engineering in its biological form blurs the distinction between generation and manufacture, between being born and being made, between being created by God and being made by man.[40] Studying people in the same way—with the same method and for the same ends—that you would study a virus or a metal objectifies and instrumentalizes what ought always to be held in reverence as made uniquely in the image of God. To deal with people as though they were mere things is the definition of oppression. Yet Bacon announces that his science, which he sold as the great benefactor of the human race, functioning as social science, will do precisely that (*NO* I.127). That's a problem.

---

39. Ibid., 64.
40. Bill Moyers, *A World of Ideas* (New York: Doubleday, 1989), 374–75.

5

REDEEMING BACON'S LEGACY: A MORE GODLY DOMINION

Bacon encouraged an attitude of hope in progress, an expectation that the future will be better than the past, and a conception of "better" that is dominated exclusively by the benefits that science can provide, whether biological, mechanical, moral, political, or economic. These are powerfully moving goals because the ills they remedy are intensely occupying. But how do we pursue these good ends without departing the kingdom of God for Bacon's rival kingdom of Man?[1]

It appears at first that Bacon had the clarity of vision to see what God has provided for fulfilling more completely our creation mandate to take dominion over the earth for the display of his glory and our commodious living. Bacon indeed saw this, though he never mentions that command. As human image bearers, this is our task of discovery: intelligently, creatively, and

---

1. Bacon introduces the body of *The New Organon* with the subtitle "Aphorisms concerning the Interpretation of Nature and the Kingdom of Man" (*Regno Homini*).

charitably unfolding and continuing God's original, six-day creative activity.

Upon closer examination, however, Bacon's project is less dominion than domination. His conquest of nature requires seeing the world in a particular way: not as creation, but as mere nature, specifically as brutally indifferent obstacle to human will, and the potential means for perfectly serving our wills and satisfying our desires. Although the Father of Salomon's House in *New Atlantis* utters pieties and, like Bacon himself, "appears all religion" when he states the purpose of his institution most definitively, and thus the purpose of science as Bacon bequeaths it to us, he says only that it is "the enlarging of the bounds of Human Empire, to the effecting of all things possible" (480). "Things" are just inert stuff without inherent purpose. Thus, at the opening of *New Atlantis*, Bacon pictures the European travelers tossed by natural forces and given up for dead, without hope in the world apart from their useless prayers. It is not God who saves them, but Bensalem, by what we later learn is its wind-controlling technology.

Yet the world, in its perfect placement, intricate operations, and astounding beauty, shouts, even sings, purposeful design.[2] In the order of the universe and of each of its parts, from the quark within us to the most distant sun, Christians—people who know the fullest reality of the world they study—see design that is not only intelligent, but also benevolent. There is neither design nor love without purpose, without *telos*. We do not understand any given thing (an object, a process, a system) until we understand not only its operation, but also its goodness, the wisdom

2. Douglas Axe, *Undeniable: How Biology Confirms Our Intuition That Life is Designed* (New York: HarperOne, 2017); Gillermo Gonzalez and Jay W. Richards, *The Privileged Planet: How Our Place in the Cosmos Is Designed for Discovery* (Washington, DC: Regnery, 2004); Geraint F. Lewis and Luke A. Barnes, *A Fortunate Universe: Life in a Finely Tuned Cosmos* (New York: Cambridge University Press, 2016); Benjamin Wiker and Jonathan Witt, *A Meaningful World: How the Arts and Sciences Reveal the Genius of Nature* (Downers Grove, IL: IVP Academic, 2006).

of its placement in the whole, not only for the functioning of the whole, but also for the blessing of the human creatures and their worship of God. Blessing is understood as more than just the temporal benefits of security and prosperity, but also our spiritual flourishing in love and in the knowledge of God. This is Christian teleology—theological, philanthropic teleology (Luke 10:27).

Of course, if there is divinely originated purpose in the natural world, then we must think differently about our wills and what we ought to desire. The modern project has made us adept at securing the basic, temporal goods of life and health. But consequently, we have come to mistake these for the only goods. We have lost sight of "that-for-the-sake-of-which." We have mistaken the means for the end. The saying "When you have your health, you have everything" is widely accepted unblinkingly as true, though given what family, friends, and higher purpose mean for virtually everyone, it is clear that no one really believes it. But Bacon encouraged us from the start to make this moral transition: to lower our sights, the better to secure the end.[3]

Gratefully accepting Bacon's God-given insights, while eschewing his hubris, requires conceptual readjustments and disciplines of the heart: humility, teleology, and theocentricity.

First, godly science must replace scientism with philosophical humility. Following Anselm, the life of the mind can be summarized as "faith seeking understanding." But that understanding does not come exclusively from science. (We can see the boastful, exclusive claim to knowledge even in the name: science—in Latin, *scientia*, knowledge or learning itself.) The method of modern science is not the only legitimate use of the human mind for grasping truths concerning this world and our life in it, not the only logic-for-truth. Science observes and

---

3. Yuval Levin, *Imagining the Future: Science and American Democracy* (New York: Encounter Books, 2008), 10–13.

analyzes the world in a particular way and for a particular end—
to discover useful information for extending our control of the
world either directly or indirectly—but the world is more than
what can be perceived that way. One can look at the world without reducing it within those terms of study.

Consider, for example, the surgeon. Surgery, along with the
understanding of the body that successful surgery requires, is
obviously useful and good. But arriving at this point of sufficient
knowledge and technique requires looking at the patient in a
particular way, in a limited respect, abstracting from all that the
patient is, but only insofar as the physician has to remove, reattach,
or correct something.[4] Otherwise, the physician—who is himself
not just a physician, but also, e.g., a husband, father, friend, citizen,
worshipper, sommelier, and fly fisherman—deals with the patient
as a whole human being. But to perform the surgery, the surgeon
must abstract from the person a merely living body. This is why
surgeons will often not operate on close family members, because
under those circumstances abstracting is more difficult.

The dignity of the legitimately contemplative life, the life of
rational inquiry into the nature of things, into what *is* as distinguished from what only *appears to be* and *is opined to be*, is not
confined to the disciplines of natural science. It extends also to
the moral, political, or social theorist, the historian, the prose or
verse poet, the theologian, the literary theorist. No individual
discipline of thought is equipped to answer all questions. This is
the error of scientism.[5]

Second, godly science must replace technology with teleology,[6] allowing a theological culture to reemerge in place of

---

4. C. S. Lewis, *The Abolition of Man* (1943; repr., New York: Macmillan, 1947),
70–71.

5. Ibid., 78–79.

6. Cornelius Van Til writes, "When God created the universe he created it for
and unto himself. By his providence God sustains the universe in order to realize his

our technological one. Christian, philanthropic, theological teleology—the explanation of things with reference to their inherent purpose, final cause, or intelligent, creational design—informs our understanding of what things are, how they came to be, and how they ought to be used, thus opening scientific research to a larger physical and moral cosmology.

This approach is fully compatible with a robust execution of the creation mandate, as we have seen in the modern age. It does not have to mean a return to the premodern, dripping pace of crude inventions. But we would unlock and apply the mysteries of the created order within the bounds of what we understand of human spiritual and moral flourishing. The technological way of looking at the world, by contrast, is a "liberation" from precisely those moral and spiritual constraints. For this reason, it is common within the scientific community to view any moral governance of their research as illegitimate, even "immoral," as by definition an intrusion of "nonscientific" direction or limitation.

The "religious Trojan horse" objection to Christian teleology is premised on what is thought to be the essential incompatibility between religion and science.[7] The subtext is that the entry of religious beliefs into scientific thinking would destroy science, admit superstition, and tempt researchers to put God into gaps like a *deus ex machina* to save the day instead of searching for natural causes.

---

ultimate purpose with it. It follows from this that there is a purpose *within* the universe because the Triune God has a purpose *for* the universe. Every purpose within the universe must, in the last analysis, be referred to God. Without this reference to God, no purpose in the universe has meaning. It follows also that every fact within the universe has a purpose, or function to fulfill. Even that which we think of as mechanical has a purpose. Mechanical laws are, from the ultimate point of view, completely teleological" (*Christian Theistic Evidences*, ed. K. Scott Oliphint [Phillipsburg, NJ: P&R Publishing, 2016], 161).

7. J. W. Draper, *History of the Conflict between Religion and Science* (1874); Andrew Dickson White, *A History of the Warfare of Science with Theology in Christendom* (1896).

What, then, does readmitting teleology into science add to the practice of science when it is producing marvelous technologies for the relief of our estate without it? First, it allows scientists to look for purpose in things, instead of overlooking what they otherwise expect to be the dead ends of undirected nature. It also allows for research that reverse engineers what we see (which many scientists do anyway). In addition, it would be a humble recognition of the limitation that science shares as a field of inquiry, a recognition that there are some things—even important things—that we can know, but not by science. For example, though it is within the competency of science to discern evidence for the necessity of a Creator (which is already accepted by faith and confirmed by ordinary experience), it is beyond its competency to explore that divine purpose in all its fullness. Thus, it properly defers to other methods of inquiry, such as theology, philosophy, philosophico-theological reflection on the historian's work, and the poetic expressions of philosophico-theological reflection.

Third, godly science must replace homocentricity with theocentricity, man-centeredness with God-centeredness. The medievals understood God as intimately involved in the natural process. He was not the divine watchmaker of eighteenth-century deism, showing up for the christening, giving it all a Big Push, and then retreating to the observation deck. A Christian view of science requires more than seeing intelligent design in the mechanisms of creation. The scientist must see what God says of himself:

He covers his hands with the lightning and commands it to strike its mark. (Job 36:32)

Ask rain from the LORD in the season of the spring rain, from the LORD who makes the storm clouds, and he will give them showers of rain, to everyone the vegetation in the field. (Zech.10:1)

For behold, he who forms the mountains and creates the wind, and declares to man what is his thought, who makes the morning darkness, and treads on the heights of the earth—the LORD, the God of hosts, is his name! (Amos 4:13)

In Psalm 147, the psalmist speaks of God equally casting down the wicked and preparing rain for the earth (vv. 6, 8). He acts in these ways by "his command" and "his word" (vv. 15, 18). We call this "providence." We speak of it. We pray for it. But we speak and pray incoherently because we do not connect our prayers and thanksgivings with our parallel and unexamined naturalistic belief in the autonomy of nature.

The language we find in the Bible was not just the way pre-modern people spoke of God, the way they spoke of his power in general, or of his capacity (should he choose) to intervene in decisive, miraculous ways, or of his sovereign decree that nature should operate in the way it does. God not only designed our world, but is intimately involved in its operations, for "he upholds the universe by the word of his power" (Heb. 1:3). God's active and intimate involvement in the operations of his universe is not limited to the miraculous and the "gaps" in our ability to explain it scientifically. He is, writes Vern Poythress, "involved in those areas where science does best."[8]

If we take the Bible at its word, we see that it teaches that God indeed sustains the world by the direct exercise of his power, operating it with a regularity that scientific observation has formulated as "laws." On this understanding, miracles occur simply when God elects to operate his creation or some locality

8. Vern Poythress, *Redeeming Science* (Wheaton, IL: Crossway, 2006), 14.

of it in a different way. An ax head floats. Water turns to wine. The dead revive. On this understanding, miracles are just what we call God's extraordinary—as opposed to his ordinary—providence.[9]

The Christian brings this understanding of an intelligent and benevolent Creator to the study of the universe. Isaac Newton (1643–1727) writes in the "General Scholium" at the end of *The Mathematical Principles of Natural Philosophy*:

> This most beautiful system of the sun, planets, and comets, could only proceed from the counsel and dominion of an intelligent and powerful Being. And if the fixed stars are the centres of other like systems, these, being formed by the like wise counsel, must be all subject to the dominion of One. . . . This Being governs all things, not as the soul of the world, but as Lord over all. . . . And from his true dominion it follows that the true God is a living, intelligent, and powerful Being; and, from his other perfections, that he is supreme, or most perfect. He is eternal and infinite, omnipotent and omniscient; that is, his duration reaches from eternity to eternity; his presence from infinity to infinity; he governs all things, and knows all things that are or can be done.

There is nothing comparable to this thorough and sincere integration of theology with natural philosophy in the writings of Francis Bacon. The Christian is someone who has been spiritually and thus intellectually and emotionally freed from hatred toward God and from the suppression of truth relating to him, and thus one who accepts the larger cosmology that

9. Westminster Shorter Catechism, 8: "Question: How doth God execute his decrees? Answer: God executeth his decrees in the works of creation and providence." Westminster Confession of Faith, 5.3: "God, in his ordinary providence, maketh use of means, yet is free to work without, above, and against them, at his pleasure."

includes God, as the Creator and Sustainer of all things, and the moral dimension of the whole. The Christian presupposes this larger cosmology and, as a scientist, confirms it by methodical investigation.

The technological society is with us from here to the far horizon, and we are unavoidably immersed in it. How then shall we live? Can technological reasoning be redeemed? Can a technological thought be made subject to Christ, or, to be so, must it no longer be technological? Are Christians forced to choose between our spiritually vacuous, technological wonderland and, as Postman puts it, "life in a godly, integrated tool-using culture," albeit burdened with hunger, disease, and oppression, presumably for oneself along with most people?[10] Surely Christian wisdom would say: Better to live a life of suffering in peace with God than to dwell in the "smart home" of the self-satisfied. "What does it profit a man to gain the whole world and forfeit his soul?" (Mark 8:36). Or can we have both? Why not a godly, technological wonderland, one might ask? This is an important and difficult question, the answer to which provides insight into the nature of technology and thus of modernity itself.

A return to premodern, tool-using culture, a hyper-Amish self-isolation, is inadvisable theologically. God has provided this world for our worshipful comfort and delight, and he commands us by his creation mandate to unlock the wonders of its riches.[11] Such a return is also practically impossible. Nora Bayes would pose her question from the Great War, "How ya gonna keep 'em down on the farm after they've seen Paree?" But the use of

---

10. Neil Postman, *Technopoly: The Surrender of Culture to Technology* (New York: Vintage, 1993), 38–39.

11. In counseling Timothy, the apostle Paul does not condemn wealth, but instead writes, "As for the rich in this present age, charge them not to be haughty, nor to set their hopes on the uncertainty of riches, but on God, who richly provides us with everything to enjoy" (1 Tim. 6:17).

inventive science for a more godly dominion calls for a few words of caution.

First and most obviously, prosperity, though good, is nonetheless a temptation to earthly-mindedness. God warned Israel at the threshold of the Promised Land, "You shall eat and be full. . . . Take care lest you forget the Lord your God" (Deut. 8:10–11). Notice that prosperity was God's promise: a land flowing with milk and honey, fat cows and fertile soil. God created us to live in the comfortable dignity suited to his image bearers and, along with that, the worshipful enjoyment of the Creator himself. But comfort separated from divine fellowship is a consuming curse, "vanity of vanities." The apostle Paul issued the same warning from his deeply pastoral heart: "The love of money is a root of all kinds of evils. It is through this craving that some have wandered away from the faith and pierced themselves with many pangs" (1 Tim. 6:10). God commanded us in Adam to take dominion over the earth, but only with God's blessing as faithful image bearers. "God blessed them. And God said to them, '. . . have dominion'" (Gen. 1:28). Rule without righteousness is Satanic rebellion, the fruits of which, though sweet in the mouth, are sour in the belly.[12] They are like the pods with which the prodigal tried to feed himself: the more he ate, the more he starved. So "godly" and "wonderland," while not mutually exclusive, sit uneasily with one another.

Second, to draw the best minds away from theology into the natural sciences and gain societal support for his project, Bacon offered hope in a beautiful, technological future. He had to convince people that what they were hoping for hereafter in the Redeemer's eschatological kingdom, and that only for some, could be achieved now in this world for all. With a controlling

---

12. David C. Innes, *Christ and the Kingdoms of Men: Foundations of Political Life* (Phillipsburg, NJ: P&R Publishing, 2019), chap. 1, "The Kingdom of God."

and productive understanding of nature, he argued, we can wipe away our own tears and dwell safely in lands flowing with much more than milk and honey. That hope still tempts and even sweeps us away. We are now living that dream, and we still have techy evangelists making the same promises of an even brighter future, even a transhuman one. This side of Bacon's conquest, it is hard to separate the earthly hope from any reconceived "technological wonderland," even a godly one.

Third, to bring us to the shores of that new continent of learning and life, much of what we understood as "reason" had to be jettisoned, retaining only what is productive to inhabiting that beautiful destination. Reason was shorn of its moral and metaphysical capacities. Science, now the only logic-for-truth, cannot reason its way to moral and metaphysical conclusions. In this way of thinking, moral and metaphysical propositions cannot be rationally verified. They can be only "values." Along with speculative and moral reasoning as forms of logic-for-truth went whole dimensions of our humanity: everything entailed in the image-bearing vice-regency of the political animal. As nice as penicillin and central heating are, they came at the cost of the rational and religious foundations for what people value most in life. Bacon, and the Enlightenment tradition that followed his lead, brought the longing soul down to earth and stuffed it to a false satiety. Thus, the basis for those dimensions of life was jettisoned in the course of our passage to the promised "technological wonderland." To reinhabit this wonderland with godly dominion, Christians must learn what technological reasoning is, repent of it, and rediscover how to think Christianly about themselves and their world, the art of moral and speculative reasoning under the authority of Scripture.[13]

13. "Modern thought reaches its culmination, its highest self-consciousness, . . . in explicitly condemning to oblivion the notion of eternity. For oblivion of eternity, or, in other words, estrangement from man's deepest desire and therewith from the

Christians will also have to adopt "living on idol alert" as their default frame of mind: "Keep yourselves from idols," wrote the aged apostle John to the nascent church (1 John 5:21). This requires strengthening three fundamental Christian disciplines pertaining to the Word of God, the church of God, and the love of God.

Know your Bible. You know a counterfeit banknote from a real one by becoming intimately familiar with real currency. Christians must equip themselves for their corrosively anti-Christian, technological world by knowing the Bible the way they know their own home. Know every level, every room, every drawer and cupboard, and the people who live there. Be rooted in the family lore and principles. Know the Bible's content and structure, its forms of literature (history, poetry, gospel, epistle, etc.) and how to read each one, its unfolding story and systematic theology. "Like newborn infants, long for the pure spiritual milk, that by it you may grow up into salvation" (1 Peter 2:2). The Scriptures must adorn our speech and illuminate our paths (Ps. 119:105). "You shall teach them diligently to your children, and shall talk of them when you sit in your house, and when you walk by the way, and when you lie down, and when you rise" (Deut. 6:7). Increasingly, our little lambs' ears will become attuned more perfectly to our Shepherd's voice, and the Scripture twisters will be seen as the wolves they are.

Root yourself in the church. The blessed man who delights in the law of the LORD and flourishes accordingly in faith is the one who centers himself not among scoffers and sinners, but among those who share his love for the kingdom of God and his righteousness (Ps. 1:1–2). He has social and commercial

---

primary issues, is the price which modern man had to pay, from the very beginning, for attempting to be absolutely sovereign, to become the master and owner of nature, to conquer chance." Leo Strauss, "What Is Political Philosophy?" in Leo Strauss, *What Is Political Philosophy? And Other Studies* (New York: The Free Press, 1959); 55.

dealings with others, but he finds friendship, community, belong-
ing, and rest among those of "like precious faith" (2 Peter 1:1
KJV). He abides in the covenant community. They are his people.
Among them, he is transformed by the renewing of his mind
(Rom. 12:2). Churches offering consumeristic worship and pro-
grams will not provide the needed counterpoise. Churches that
present themselves as "cutting edge" or "relevant" or "creative"
or (heaven forbid) "progressive" remain sunk in the Baconian
project and will not help their disciples extricate themselves from
the Baconian problems: scientistic reasoning and the technological culture of human autonomy and boundless possibilities. But
Christ-centered, biblically serious churches, rooted historically
in confessional and liturgical tradition, including the Psalter and
historic hymnody, will disciple Christ's people in a faith that
stands against whatever in the modern world stands against
the faith.

Center yourself in love. Love must become ever more perfectly
our central concern. Love draws one out of oneself. It turns one's
eyes away from immediate and oh-so-temporal concerns (legitimate though at times they may be) and redirects them toward
others in their temporal and eternal concerns. "Love is patient and
kind" (1 Cor. 13:4) because love is self-forgetting, self-sacrificing,
and other-focused. It is not technological, is not efficient,[14] but
always hopes. Love will lay down its life for a friend and, in the
confidence of God's love in Christ, will serve even an enemy.
Love seeks first the kingdom of God and his righteousness, and
it leaves "what you shall wear and what you shall eat" in second
place. Love also labors for food and clothing and shelter—the
things modern, industrial science is good at providing in ever
greater and better abundance—but labors to provide not so much

---

14. D. C. Innes, "The Inefficiency of Love," in *The Voting Christian* (Lindenhurst,
NY: Great Christian Books, 2016), 64–66.

for oneself as for others: one's family, one's church, and strangers within one's reasonable sphere of provision.

With Christians strengthened and sanctified in these disciplines, theological culture would begin significantly to displace the technological, and Francis Bacon's legacy of autonomous, human domination would turn to the worshipful, saintly dominion that God gave Bacon his genius to serve.

GLOSSARY

Adam and Eve Pools. In *New Atlantis,* a Bensalemite arrangement to facilitate marital stability by permitting one's friend to view a prospective mate bathing and alert him or her about any potentially displeasing blemish.

agape. Greek: love.

aphorism. The short, pithy, memorable expression of a point. Bacon recommended writing by aphorism and short essays "in tender matters and ticklish times" when men must "beware what they say." These "fly abroad like darts, and are thought to be shot out of their secret intentions." Essay No. 15, "Of Seditions and Troubles."

atomism. The theory held by the pre-Socratic philosopher Democritus (fifth century B.C.) that everything consists of atoms—small, indivisible particles—and thus that happiness is the proper arrangement of atoms in the soul.

autonomy. As a moral quality attributed to individual human beings by modern political theory, not only self-government but also having authority within oneself and thus being accountable only to oneself.

axiom. A conclusion or general hypothesis regarding the nature and operation of the world drawn only from methodologically observed particulars.

Bensalem. Bacon's fictional island home of scientific civilization in *New Atlantis.*

cause, efficient. The external agent of change.

cause, final. That toward which a thing is ordered, whether externally or internally; the "that for the sake of which" (Aristotle).

civil. Fitted for or subordinate to the needs of peaceful, efficiently functioning society.

creation mandate. God's command to all his human creatures to rule over his creation in his name. Also known as the cultural mandate or the dominion mandate.

deism. Belief in a supreme being who, as a first cause, created the universe but does not intervene in it, either in human affairs or in natural processes.

deus ex machina. Latin: lit. "god from the machinery," a reference to a device used on the ancient Greek stage by which a god would enter the drama just in time to solve a difficulty.

dissimulation. Denying what is true of you. From Essay No. 6: "There be three degrees of this hiding and veiling of a man's self. . . . The second, dissimulation, in the negative; when a man lets fall signs and arguments, that he is not, that he is."

ecumenical. Representing broad, interdenominational Christianity or even the worldwide church.

empiricism. The philosophic theory, in disagreement with rationalism, that knowledge comes solely by sense experience.

Enlightenment. The philosophic movement of the seventeenth and eighteenth centuries that elaborated an understanding of life and the universe based on reason alone; a form of rationalism, in contradistinction to what it saw as the moral and intellectual darkness of medieval, Christian civilization.

Epicureanism. The naturalistic and often atheistic philosophy beginning with Epicurus (341–270 B.C.) that viewed pleasure as the highest good, albeit the high pleasure of philosophical understanding.

epistemology. A branch of philosophy that investigates how one can know and be certain that one knows.

eugenics. The science of human improvement by controlled breeding for the selection of desirable inherited qualities.

experience. Within the context of Bacon's epistemology, observation mediated by the discipline of proper inductive method.

Feast of the Family. In *New Atlantis,* a state-sponsored festival celebrating "any man that shall live to see thirty persons descended of his body, alive together, and all above three years old."

form. The internal operation of causes that make a thing appear and operate as it does.

general revelation. God's self-disclosure to people in all places and in every age by rational reflection on the creation.

hope. A confident expectation of some good.

hope-as-goal. Some future good that one confidently expects to obtain and enjoy; in the Baconian context, broadly enjoyed comfort and security through the human control of all things.

hope-as-method. The reliable means by which one confidently expects some good to be obtained and enjoyed; in the Baconian context, the modern method of scientific inquiry into the operations of nature with a view to the human control of all things.

human exceptionalism. The view that human beings have unique value in the universe.

humanity. As distinguished from Christian charity, the benevolent disposition to provide others with comfort and security, embracing the toleration and civility of religious and civil peace.

idol. In Bacon's use of the word, a way by which "the human intellect makes its own difficulties" in understanding the world (*NO* I.38–68).

image of God. The human creature's righteousness and rule as vice-regent over the creation.

imago dei. Latin: image of God.

induction. Reasoning from particular observations in experience to general conclusions or hypotheses.

instauratio. Latin: instauration. See instauration.

instauration (*instauratio*). A term taken from the Vulgate, Jerome's fourth-century translation of the Bible into Latin, suggesting both a restoration and a new beginning.

logic-for-persuasion. The method of reason suited for changing people's minds or winning their hearts.

logic-for-truth. The method of reason for accessing and ascertaining what is so.

logos. Greek: a word with a wide lexical range, meaning everything from "word" and "announcement" to "reason" and "argument."

Lord Chancellor. The highest executive position in the English royal government; the head of the judiciary, responsible for overseeing the integrity and operation of the courts and responsible also for overseeing the House of Lords.

Machiavellian. One who follows the teachings of Niccolò Machiavelli (1469–1527), a Renaissance diplomat, historian, and political theorist known for his amoral, unscrupulous approach to statecraft; one who practices the politics of expedience.

metaphysics. "First philosophy"; philosophical inquiry into first principles, such as being, essence, change, "first causes and the principles of things" (Aristotle); often, the study of that which transcends or grounds empirical reality.

natural history. The record of observations from experiments from which axioms are derived.

naturalism, philosophical. A view of the world that excludes the supernatural or spiritual, and thus the insistence that the world operates only by, and is thus wholly explicable in terms of, natural laws and forces.

organum. Latin: tool, instrument; for Bacon, a method of reasoning or logic.

proemium (or proem). A preamble, preface, or introduction.

progress. Advancement in the conquest of nature for broadly enjoyed comfort and security.

rationalism. The philosophical theory that reason, as distinguished from tradition or divine revelation, is the sole basis of knowledge. A second sense of the term, used in contradistinction to empiricism, holds that the foundation of knowledge is reason, not sense experience.

Renfusa. In *New Atlantis,* the capital city of Bacon's fictional island, Bensalem.

Salomon's House. In *New Atlantis,* the institution of scientific research and development that is "the very eye of this kingdom."

scientism. The exclusivity of natural science as a way of knowing.

shalom. Hebrew: peace. Its depth of meaning includes peace with God in grace, with oneself in good conscience, with one another in love, and with the world in faithful vice-regency.

simulation. Affirming what is not true of you. From Essay No. 6: "There be three degrees of this hiding and veiling of a man's self. . . . And the third, simulation, in the affirmative; when a man industriously and expressly feigns and pretends to be, that he is not."

Social Darwinism. The application of Charles Darwin's principles of natural selection—the survival of the fittest—to social betterment or even simply to personal power and prosperity.

Strangers' House. In *New Atlantis*, a public institution in Bensalem established to extend hospitality to foreign travelers who happen upon the island despite the ancient law forbidding the entry of outsiders.

summum bonum. Latin: ultimate good.

summum malum. Latin: ultimate evil.

techne. Greek: the art or skill of producing something.

technocracy. Rule by technocrats, technically trained specialists, on the authority of their expertise.

technological society. A society that is impatient with the present, happy to be free of the past, and hopeful for the future, based primarily on the history of unfolding benefits from technology; a society completely open to possibility.

technology. The modern marriage of *techne* and *logos* that places reason solely in the service of making; a way of thinking about the world that instrumentalizes everything with human autonomy set over the world as the object of will.

teleology. The explanation of things with reference to their inherent purpose, final cause, or intelligent design.

telos. Greek: end, purpose, or goal.

theological society. A society in which the accepted metaphysical and moral beliefs and the authorities responsible for curating them set boundaries for invention and the use of what is invented.

thumos. Greek: the competitive desire for personal distinction; the warrior spirit; the seat of both anger and shame.

totalitarianism. Oppressive government that not only holds total power, but also, on account of modern technology, exercises total control.

transhumanism. The movement to take intelligent, technological control of human evolution.

vice-regency. Service in kingly rule under a high king in his place; the office to which all human beings are appointed by God as image bearers in taking "dominion over the earth" (Gen. 1:26–28).

BIBLIOGRAPHY

Primary Sources

Bacon, Francis. *Essayes or Counsels, Civill and Morall.* Edited by Michael Kiernan. Cambridge, MA: Harvard University Press, 1985.

_____. *The Major Works.* Edited by Brian Vickers. New York: Oxford University Press, 2002.

_____. *The Oxford Francis Bacon.* Edited by Graham Rees. Oxford: Oxford University Press, 1998.

_____. *Selected Philosophical Works.* Edited by Rose-Mary Sargent. Indianapolis: Hackett, 1999.

_____. *The Works of Francis Bacon.* Edited by James Spedding, Robert Leslie Ellis, and Douglas Denon Heath. London: Longmans, 1870.

Farrington, Benjamin. *The Philosophy of Francis Bacon: An Essay on Its Development from 1603 to 1609 with New Translations of Fundamental Texts.* Chicago: University of Chicago Press, 1966.

Fowler, Thomas, ed. *Bacon's Novum Organum.* 2nd ed. Oxford: Clarendon Press, 1889.

Secondary Works

Aeschliman, Michael D. *The Restitution of Man: C.S. Lewis and the Case Against Scientism*. Grand Rapids: Eerdmans, 1983.

Aristotle, *Nicomachean Ethics*. Translated by Robert C. Bartlett and Susan D. Collins. Chicago: University of Chicago Press, 2011.

Aubrey, John. *Brief Lives*. Edited by John Buchanan-Brown. London: Penguin, 2000.

Axe, Douglas. *Undeniable: How Biology Confirms Our Intuition That Life Is Designed*. New York: HarperOne, 2017.

Berns, Laurence. "Francis Bacon and the Conquest of Nature." *Interpretation* 7, no. 1 (1978): 1–26.

Blanning, Tim. *The Pursuit of Glory: The Five Revolutions That Made Modern Europe: 1648–1815*. New York: Penguin, 2007.

Box, Ian. *The Social Thought of Francis Bacon*. New York: Edwin Mellen, 1989.

Bozeman, Theodore Dwight. *Protestants in an Age of Science: The Baconian Ideal and Antebellum American Religious Thought*. Chapel Hill: University of North Carolina Press, 1977.

Briggs, John C. *Francis Bacon and the Rhetoric of Nature*. Cambridge, MA: Harvard University Press, 1989.

Broad, C. D. *The Philosophy of Francis Bacon*. 1926; repr., New York: Octagon, 1976.

Bultmann, Rudolf. *The New Testament and Mythology and Other Basic Writings*. Edited and translated by Schubert M. Ogden. Philadelphia: Fortress, 1984.

Butterfield, Herbert. *The Origins of Modern Science, 1300–1800*. Rev. ed. New York: Free Press, 1965.

Churchill, Winston S. "Fifty Years Hence." In *Thoughts and Adventures*. 1932; repr., New York: W. W. Norton, 1991.

Cohen, Eric. *In the Shadow of Progress: Being Human in the Age of Technology*. New York: Encounter Books, 2008.

Craig, Tobin L. "On the Significance of the Literary Character of Francis Bacon's *New Atlantis* for an Understanding of His Political Thought." *Review of Politics* 72, no. 2 (2010): 213–39.

Crowther, J. G. *Francis Bacon: The First Statesman of Science.* London: Cresset, 1960.

Darwin, Charles. *The Autobiography of Charles Darwin.* Edited by Nora Barlow. New York: Norton, 1969.

———. *The Descent of Man.* Repr., New York: Penguin, 2004.

Dewey, John. *Reconstruction in Philosophy.* New York: Henry Holt, 1920.

Eiseley, Loren. *Francis Bacon and the Modern Dilemma.* New York: Charles Scribner's Sons, 1973.

Eliot, T. S. *The Use of Poetry and the Use of Criticism.* Cambridge, MA: Harvard University Press, 1933.

Ellul, Jacques. *The Technological Society.* Translated by John Wilkinson. New York: Vintage, 1964.

Farrington, Benjamin. *Francis Bacon, Philosopher of Industrial Science.* London: Lawrence and Wishart, 1951.

Faulkner, Robert K. *Francis Bacon and the Project of Progress.* Lanham, MD: Rowman & Littlefield, 1993.

Fischer, Kuno. *Francis Bacon of Verulam: Realistic Philosophy and Its Age.* London: Longman, Brown, Green, 1857.

Gaukroger, Stephen. *Francis Bacon and the Transformation of Early-Modern Philosophy.* Cambridge: Cambridge University Press, 2001.

Gonzalez, Gillermo, and Jay W. Richards, *The Privileged Planet: How Our Place in the Cosmos Is Designed for Discovery.* Washington: Regnery, 2004.

Gordon, Bruce L., and William A. Dembski, eds. *The Nature of Nature: Examining the Role of Naturalism in Science.* Wilmington, DE: ISI Books, 2011.

Grant, Edward. *The Foundations of Modern Science in the Middle Ages.* Cambridge: Cambridge University Press, 1996.

Grant, George. "'The Computer Does Not Impose on Us the Ways It Should Be Used.'" In *The George Grant Reader*, edited by William Christian and Sheila Grant, 418–34. Toronto: University of Toronto Press, 1998.

———. *Technology and Empire*. Toronto: House of Anansi, 1969.

Harper, Lisa Sharon, and D. C. Innes. *Left, Right, and Christ*. Boise, ID: Russell Media, 2011.

Heidegger, Martin. *The Question concerning Technology and Other Essays*. Translated by William Lovitt. New York: Harper & Row, 1977.

Innes, David C. "Bacon's *New Atlantis*: The Christian Hope and the Modern Hope." *Interpretation* 22, 1 (1994): 3–37.

———. "Bacon's *New Atlantis*: The Christian Hope and the Modern Hope." In *Piety and Humanity: Essays on Religion and Early Modern Political Philosophy*, edited by Douglas Kries, 49–77. Lanham, MD: Rowman & Littlefield, 1997.

———. *Christ and the Kingdoms of Men: Foundations of Political Life*. Phillipsburg, NJ: P&R Publishing, 2019.

———. "Civil Religion as Political Technology in Bacon's *New Atlantis*." In *Civil Religion in Political Thought*, edited by Ronald Weed and John von Heyking, 121–44. Washington: Catholic University of America Press, 2010.

———. "Francis Bacon." In *Religion and Politics in America: An Encyclopedia of Church and State in American Life*, edited by Frank J. Smith, 1:45–46. Santa Barbara, CA: ABC-CLIO, 2016.

———. *The Voting Christian: Seeking Wisdom for the Ballot Box*. Lindenhurst, NY: Great Christian Books, 2016.

Jaki, Stanley. *The Road of Science and the Ways to God*. Chicago: University of Chicago Press, 1978.

Jardine, Lisa, and Alan Stewart. *Hostage to Fortune: The Troubled Life of Francis Bacon*. New York: Hill and Wang, 1999.

Jonas, Hans. *The Phenomenon of Life: Toward a Philosophical Biology*. New York: Harper & Row, 1966.

Kass, Leon. *Life, Liberty and the Defense of Dignity: The Challenge for Bioethics*. San Francisco: Encounter Books, 2002.

———. *Toward a More Natural Biology: Biology and Human Affairs*. New York: Free Press, 1985.

Kennington, Richard. *On Modern Origins: Essays in Early Modern Philosophy*. Edited by Pamela Kraus and Frank Hunt. Lanham, MD: Lexington Books, 2004.

Lampert, Laurence. *Nietzsche and Modern Times: A Study of Bacon, Descartes, and Nietzsche*. New Haven: Yale University Press, 1993.

Levin, Yuval. *Imagining the Future: Science and American Democracy*. New York: Encounter Books, 2008.

———. *Tyranny of Reason: The Origin and Consequences of the Social Scientific Outlook*. Lanham, MD: University Press of America, 2001.

Lewis, C. S. *The Abolition of Man*. 1943; repr., New York: Macmillan, 1947.

———. *Christian Reflections*. Grand Rapids: Eerdmans, 1967.

———. *Miracles*. 1947; repr., Glasgow: Collins, 1960.

———. *That Hideous Strength*. 1945; repr., New York: Scribner, 2003.

Lewis, Geraint F., and Luke A. Barnes, *A Fortunate Universe: Life in a Finely Tuned Cosmos*. New York: Cambridge University Press, 2016.

Lindberg, David C. *The Beginnings of Western Science*. 2nd ed. Chicago: University of Chicago Press, 2007.

Lindberg, David C., and Ronald L. Numbers, eds. *God and Nature: Historical Essays on the Encounter between Christianity and Science*. Berkeley: University of California Press, 1986.

Machen, J. Gresham. *Christianity and Liberalism*. 1923; repr., Grand Rapids: Eerdmans, 1946.

Manuel, Frank, and Fritzie Manuel. *Utopian Thought in the Western World.* Cambridge, MA: Belknap Press, 1979.

McCloskey, Deirdre. *Bourgeois Equality: How Ideas, Not Capital or Institutions, Enriched the World.* Chicago: University of Chicago Press, 2016.

McKnight, Stephen A. *The Religious Foundations of Francis Bacon's Thought.* Columbia, MO: University of Missouri Press, 2006.

Melzer, Arthur M. *Philosophy between the Lines: The Lost History of Esoteric Writing.* Chicago: University of Chicago Press, 2014.

Melzer, Arthur M., Jerry Weinberger, and M. Richard Zinman, eds. *Technology in the Western Political Tradition.* Ithaca, NY: Cornell University Press, 1993.

Minkov, Svetozar Y. *Francis Bacon's "Inquiry Touching Human Nature": Virtue, Philosophy, and the Relief of Man's Estate.* Lanham, MD: Lexington Books, 2010.

Morrison, James C. "Philosophy and History in Bacon." *Journal of the History of Ideas* 38 (1977): 585–606.

Moyers, Bill. *A World of Ideas.* New York: Doubleday, 1989.

Newbigin, Lesslie. *Foolishness to the Greeks.* Grand Rapids: Eerdmans, 1986.

Paterson, Timothy H. "Bacon's Myth of Orpheus: Power as a Goal of Science in *Of the Wisdom of the Ancients.*" *Interpretation* 16, no. 3 (1989): 427–44.

———. "On the Role of Christianity in the Political Philosophy of Francis Bacon." *Polity* 19, no. 3 (1987): 419–42.

Pearcey, Nancy. *Total Truth: Liberating Christianity from Its Cultural Captivity.* Wheaton, IL: Crossway, 2004.

Pearcey, Nancy, and Charles B. Thaxton. *The Soul of Science: Christian Faith and Natural Philosophy.* Wheaton, IL: Crossway, 1994.

Peltonen, Markku, ed. *The Cambridge Companion to Bacon*. Cambridge: Cambridge University Press, 1996.

Perez-Ramos, Antonio. *Francis Bacon's Idea of Science and the Maker's Knowledge Tradition*. Oxford: Oxford University Press, 1988.

Pesic, Peter. "Desire, Science, and Polity: Francis Bacon's Account of Eros." *Interpretation* 26, no. 3 (1999): 333–52.

———. "Wrestling with Proteus: Francis Bacon and the 'Torture' of Nature." *ISIS* 90 (1999): 81–94.

Pinker, Steven. *Enlightenment Now: The Case for Reason, Science, Humanism, and Progress*. New York: Viking, 2018.

Postman, Neil. *Technopoly: The Surrender of Culture to Technology*. New York: Vintage, 1993.

Powell, James M., ed. *Medieval Studies: An Introduction*. 2nd ed. Syracuse, NY: Syracuse University Press, 1992.

Poythress, Vern S. *Redeeming Science: A God-Centered Approach*. Wheaton, IL: Crossway, 2006.

Price, Bronwen, ed. *Francis Bacon's New Atlantis: New Interdisciplinary Essays*. Manchester: Manchester University Press, 2002.

Rossi, Paolo. *Francis Bacon: From Magic to Science*. Chicago: University of Chicago Press, 1968.

———. *Philosophy, Technology, and the Arts in the Early Modern Era*. Translated by Salvator Attanasio. New York: Harper & Row, 1970.

Rubin, Charles T. *Eclipse of Man*. New York: Encounter Books, 2014.

Skinner, B. F. *Beyond Freedom and Dignity*. New York: Bantam Books, 1972.

Smith, Wesley J. *A Rat Is a Pig Is a Dog Is a Boy*. New York: Encounter Books, 2010.

———. *The War on Humans*. Seattle: Discovery Institute Press, 2014.

Stark, Rodney. *For the Glory of God: How Monotheism Led to Reformations, Science, Witch-Hunts, and the End of Slavery.* Princeton: Princeton University Press, 2004.

Strachey, Lytton. *Elizabeth and Essex: A Tragic History.* New York: Harcourt Brace, 1928.

Strauss, Leo. *What Is Political Philosophy? And Other Studies.* New York: The Free Press, 1959.

Studer, Heidi D. "'Cross Your Heart and Hope to Die?' Francis Bacon on Making and Breaking Promises." *Interpretation* 28, no. 1 (2000): 3–15.

———. "Francis Bacon on the Political Dangers of Scientific Progress." *Canadian Journal of Political Science* 31 (1998): 219–34.

———. "Francis Bacon: Philosopher or Ideologue?" *Review of Politics* 59 (1997): 915–26.

Tocqueville, Alexis de. *Democracy in America.* Edited by J. P. Mayer. Translated by George Lawrence. Garden City, NY: Anchor, 1969.

Tuchman, Barbara W. *A Distant Mirror: The Calamitous 14th Century.* New York: Ballantine Books, 1978.

Van Malssen, Tom. *The Political Philosophy of Francis Bacon: On the Unity of Knowledge.* Albany, NY: SUNY Press, 2015.

Van Til, Cornelius. *Christian Theistic Evidences.* Edited by K. Scott Oliphint. Phillipsburg, NJ: P&R Publishing, 2016.

Voegelin, Eric. *The New Science of Politics.* Chicago: University of Chicago Press, 1952.

Voltaire, *Letters concerning the English Nation.* Edited by Nicholas Cronk. Oxford: Oxford University Press, 1999.

Webster, Charles. *The Great Instauration: Science, Medicine, and Reform, 1626–1660.* London: Duckworth, 1975.

Weikart, Richard. *From Darwin to Hitler: Evolutionary Ethics, Eugenics, and Racism in Germany.* New York: Palgrave Macmillan, 2004.

Weinberger, Jerry. "Science and Rule in Bacon's Utopia." *American Political Science Review* 70 (1976): 865–85.

———. *Science, Faith, and Politics: Francis Bacon and the Utopian Roots of the Modern Age.* Ithaca, NY: Cornell University Press, 1985.

West, John G. *Darwin Day in America: How Our Politics and Culture Have Been Dehumanized in the Name of Science.* Wilmington, DE: ISI Books, 2007.

———, ed. *The Magician's Twin: C. S. Lewis on Science, Scientism, and Society.* Seattle: Discovery Institute Press, 2012.

Weston, Paul, ed. *Lesslie Newbigin: Missionary Theologian: A Reader.* Grand Rapids: Eerdmans, 2006.

White, Howard B. *Antiquity Forgot: Essays on Shakespeare, Bacon, and Rembrandt.* The Hague: Martinus Nijhoff, 1978.

———. "Bacon's Imperialism." *American Political Science Review* 52, no. 2 (1958): 470–89.

———. "Bacon's *Wisdom of the Ancients*." *Interpretation* 1, no. 2 (1970): 107–29.

———. "The English Solomon: Francis Bacon on Henry VII." *Social Research* 24 (1957): 457–81.

———. "Francis Bacon." In *History of Political Philosophy*, edited by Leo Strauss and Joseph Cropsey, 340–59. 3rd ed. Chicago: University of Chicago Press, 1987.

———. *Peace among the Willows: The Political Philosophy of Francis Bacon.* The Hague: Martinus Nijhoff, 1968.

Whitehead, Alfred North. *Science and the Modern World.* New York: Free Press, 1967.

Whitney, Charles. *Francis Bacon and Modernity.* New Haven: Yale University Press, 1986.

———. "Francis Bacon's *Instauratio*: Dominion of and over Humanity." *Journal of the History of Ideas* 50 (1989): 371–90.

Wiker, Benjamin, and Jonathan Witt. *A Meaningful World: How the Arts and Sciences Reveal the Genius of Nature*. Downers Grove, IL: IVP Academic, 2006.

Wormald, B. H. G. *Francis Bacon: History, Politics, and Science, 1561–1626*. Cambridge: Cambridge University Press, 1993.

Zagorin, Perez. *Francis Bacon*. Princeton: Princeton University Press, 1998.

INDEX OF SCRIPTURE

INDEX OF SUBJECTS
AND NAMES

David C. Innes (PhD, Boston College; MDiv, Reformed Presbyterian Theological Seminary) is professor of politics and chairman of the Program in Politics, Philosophy, and Economics at The King's College in New York City. His scholarly research has focused on the political philosophy of Francis Bacon, with articles in *Interpretation: A Journal of Political Philosophy* (1993), *Piety and Humanity*, edited by Douglas Kries (Lanham, MD: Rowman & Littlefield, 1997), and *Civil Religion in Political Thought*, edited by Ronald Weed and John von Heyking (Washington: Catholic University of America Press, 2010). He has written on current politics in *The Washington Times*, HuffingtonPost.com, American Thinker, The Daily Caller, and Worldmag.com, where he wrote a weekly column from 2010 to 2016. He is the author of *Christ and the Kingdoms of Men: Foundations of Political Life* (Phillipsburg, NJ: P&R Publishing, 2019) and *The Voting Christian: Seeking Wisdom for the Ballot Box* (2016), and the coauthor of *Left, Right, and Christ: Evangelical Faith in Politics* (2011). He is an ordained minister in the Orthodox Presbyterian Church and lives on Long Island, New York, with his wife and four children.

Did you find this book helpful?
Consider writing a review online.
The author appreciates your feedback!

Or write to P&R at editorial@prpbooks.com
with your comments. We'd love to hear from you.